RANTS

RAVES

AND

REPRISALS

Columns from the Morning Star
by **Paddy McGuffin**

Published by People's Press Printing Society Ltd
52 Beachy Road, London E3
www.morningstaronline.co.uk

Edited by James Eagle

ISBN: 978-0-9541473-2-7

Contents

hearing I had reluctantly decided to rule
sheer enormity of Blair's smugness and me
form of chain reaction causing a conflagrati
and therefore an unwitting act of self-immo

did was try to link September 11 to the Ir
ular claim didn't hold water eight years a
evidence to support this egregious claim be

were carried out mainly by

urprise, surprise. Tony Blair thinks he wa
illion people in an illegal war because he
e was right.

ell, that was worth £250k of public money
nows how much in inquiry salaries, wasn't

arles Manson probably eally honestly bel:
every egomania   derer in

Tories & Toffs

y'll probably be entitled "How to shaft ab
e yourself."

Blair was always going to allow his messi
—yet again.

Right up

Meryl Streep won glowing reviews elsewhere in the press for The Iron Lady-- but although depicting Thatcher's 'human side' was a feat on a par with scaling Everest it was a poor time to try rehabilitating the former PM with revelations she planned to abandon Liverpool to decay

Beyond caricature

JEFF SAWTELL reveals the motives behind a revisionist, Oscar-friendly view of Margaret Thatcher

Morning Star

THATCHER EXPOSED: P3   Secret plans for mass detentions, militarised police, her shady parliamentary deals and nuclear madness

Talks roll to end tyre firm lock-out

Occupy has roots in the Depression

LIVERPOOL? LET 'EM ROT

How vindictive Tory ministers planned to abandon city to decline in wake of '81 riots

Thierry Henry set for Arsenal return

Reinvention—or, to be more accurate, rehashing—is very much the order of the day. You can't turn on a TV or go to your local cinema without having the latest remake of Mission Impossible, The Girl with the Dragon Tattoo and pretty much everything Michael Caine was ever in shoved down your gullet.

Basically the key to success in the movies these days seems to be to churn out anything that requires zero imagination or effort, something that can be slapped together in a couple of weeks with a minimal script and loads of CGI effects chucked at it, and it will generate gazillions of pounds from the pockets of the gullible public.

Then flog the idea until it's dead with interminable sequels until any shred of creativity or artistry accidentally conveyed in the original has been sucked dry. If they can make it 3D and flog you a pair of glasses for an extra tenner, all to the better.

Genghis Khan: The Mongol Who Loved Me, Armageddon II (This Time It's Really Over) and Buffy the Investment Banker Slayer. You name it, they WILL make it. Actually I wouldn't mind seeing that last one, but you get the point.

And if you can't even be bothered to do that, just go through your DVD collection and remake one of those badly.

TV is exactly the same—for every original thought-provoking drama there are a dozen hacks preferring to replunder the works of Dickens, Austen and the Brontës.

Because, let's face it, what the world really needs is a new version of Pride and Prejudice with the fop de jour poncing around as Mr Darcy to launch his movie career.

There have been glowing reviews over the festive period of the performance by a respected Hollywood star in the latest "interpretation" of a bitter old harpy hellbent on destroying the happiness of others and who finally goes completely insane.

And then there was Gillian Anderson's acclaimed performance as Miss Haversham in Great Expectations.

This column has not watched—and has no intention of bothering to—the new Thatcher biopic starring Meryl Streep in which the one-time star of Silkwood and Out of Africa assumes the role of the eponymous harridan.

Streep has been reported as saying she attempted to show the "human side" of Margaret Thatcher. Talk about setting yourself a challenge.

You couldn't find her human side with an exorcist and a bottle of holy water. You'd have more chance of reinventing Rupert Murdoch as that loveable leather-skinned larrikin Crocodile Dundee.

But the rehabilitation of Thatcher has become a growth industry in recent years. They'll be bringing out action figures soon.

Normally people have to die to be the subject of such blatantly hagiographical revisionism. Either that or be the Pope, or a fascist sympathiser and/or member of the house of Windsor.

From Gordon Brown inviting her to Number 10 and posing for obsequious photographs with the old bat, to not just one but two biopics. You can't walk down the street these days without seeing her image, as channelled by Streep.

The spin put on the recent Cabinet document disclosures under the 30-year rule from certain quarters was phenomenal. Various commentators attempted to claim they showed the sensitive, compassionate side of a PM resisting pressure from her Cabinet to let Liverpool rot. This of course is conveniently forgetting that that's exactly what her government did not just to Merseyside but the entire north of England.

Then there are the disgraceful ongoing attempts to have her honoured with a state funeral so that we'll be paying for her even after she finally dies.

Personally my vote's on having her interred at the bottom of an abandoned coalmine.

I'm sure it's what she would have wanted.

as right to kill up 1
"really honestly" believe

A right-wing

lay
cha
r s
rtm

decided to rule out
r's smugness and me:
ausing a conflagrat:
ng act of self-immo

fel
hir
be

nting the possibili
and confess all, re
he rest of

is
ici

Feet in mouths all round as Tory peer Lord Young lost his job for telling us we 'had never had it so good' in this 'so-called recession' but Ukip's Godfrey Bloom managed to keep his despite calling a German MEP a nazi

eek
th
pop
ks

bab
elf.

was

hose
not
on

thir

tember 11 to the 1

icul

ight years ago.

this egregious c

s ... on probably really ho...tly believed he was right to ...sn't ...they
gaffeathon
trigger some form of chain reaction cau... ...agratio
...t and therefore an unwitting act of self-immola

It's been a week of ill-advised opinion-spouting, often in spectacularly self-immolatory fashion. First we had Lord Young telling us we should stop whingeing about the recession and that in a few years everyone would wonder what all the fuss was about.

As public acts of hara-kiri go this was up there with Japanese aesthete author Yukio Mishima, although probably not as intentional.

The furore surrounding Young's facetious comments ensured that his career took the ejector seat option and caused major embarrassment to David Cameron who—ahem— "accepted" the peer's resignation while praising his vicious slash-and-burn review of health and safety as absolutely spiffing.

But as we all know, the true heavyweight champion when it comes to foot-in-mouth syndrome is the UK Independence Party—and none more so than Yorkshire and North Lincolnshire MEP Godfrey Bloom. Perhaps fearing a contender to his undisputed crown, Bloom came out fighting in jaw-dropping fashion, even by his standards.

At a meeting of the European Parliament on Wednesday Bloom interrupted a speech by German Social Democrat Martin Schulz by braying: "Ein Volk, ein Reich, ein Führer."

Schulz was understandably quite annoyed by this comment, perhaps particularly as he has been subjected to such a slur before, when Silvio Berlusconi in one of his more outlandish utterances in 2003 referred to the hapless German as looking like a concentration camp guard.

For an Italian to make jokes about another country's fascist past is a bit rich, especially a right-wing Italian with views on immigration akin to those of Il Duce himself. Berlusconi of course did not apologise for his remarks and neither did Bloom.

Perhaps the sheer hypocrisy of representing a virulently anti-European party—in fact some would say that was Ukip's only policy—in the European Parliament is taking its toll on him. But probably not…

This is a man who in 2004 stated that "no small businessman with a brain would ever employ a lady of child-bearing age," adding bizarrely that women did not "clean behind the fridge enough."

On being expelled from the chamber Bloom, showing he is not even on nodding terms with the concept of irony, said: "These Euro-nationalists are a danger to democracy. These people are fanatics. People have got to wake up to this fact."

Ukip leader Nigel Farage, the Isadora Duncan of aerial electioneering, also defended the remarks. "Whereas we accept that Mr Bloom's jibe in the parliament may have been rash and inflammatory, we fully support his sentiments about the formation of an undemocratic Europe," he said.

But all of the above was knocked into a cocked hat by the comments of Howard Flight, one of the new batch of Tory peers anointed by Cameron this week.

Flight, apparently having chafed at the faux-liberal bit for too long, claimed that cuts to child benefit for high earners would be an incentive for the poor to breed.

We know the Tories are all thinking these things, but it

takes a real bellowing buffoon to say it so blatantly and, flying in the face of fashion, not even on Twitter which some wag recently described as "people with nothing to say, saying it in 140 characters or less."

Flight, an ex-banker—surprise surprise—seemed to have got the cart before the horse somewhat though.

Everyone knows the Lords has more than its fair share of geriatric bigots who say that kind of thing day in day out and would probably call for forced sterilisation of anyone earning less than £60,000.

Once you get into the Lords there's basically only one way of getting you out—feet first. Crucially though you do have to get there first ... and beat Lord Tebbit to it.

February 4 2012

-----

is right to kill up 1
"really honestly" believed

Septic

GPs URGE PM: SCRAP HEALTH BILL BEFORE IT'S TOO LATE

Toxic
Tories
and
laughable
Lib Dems
slugged
it out to see
who was the
most deluded.
Andrew
Lansley gave
it his best shot
with his insane NHS
'reforms', William
Hague and
David
Cameron
talked
tough and
acted feeble on
foreign policy,
Chris Huhne
protested his
innocence to the
end--but there
was only ever going
to be one winner

decided to rule ou
r's smugness and me
ausing a conflagrat
ng act of self-immo

nting the possibili
and confess all, re
devote the rest of

EU AUSTERITY
Skinner slams PM's Europe capitulation
Labour MP says Cameron has sold out working classes across EU

he stand at an inqu
he Hague, he took a
d Lansdowne Partner

absolutely everyor

ssianic tendencies

TAXI FOR HUHNE
Energy secretary resigns after being hit with criminal charge

g at his blatant h

FALKLANDS DISPUTE
Argentina condemns warship deployment
Prince William despatched to islands 'in conquistador uniform' – government

ight years ago.

this egregious c

was

hose
not
on

thi

icul

probably really ho...tly believed he was right to...
...n't... they
...l mass...

tankers

trigger some form of chain reaction cau...
...therefore an unwitting act of self-immola...

One has to marvel at the sheer capacity for self-delusion exhibited so readily by the denizens of this septic isle—and its self-styled leaders in particular. This has been a bumper week.

We have a Health Secretary hell-bent on "reforming" the NHS when even the GPs he wants to hand it over to have told him his policies are insane.

Andrew Lansley has had an effect on the NHS roughly equivalent to that of MRSA, except that you can't get rid of him with a thorough washing of your hands. Which when you think about is ironic because hand-washing is pretty much the only consistent coalition policy these days.

Then of course there's David Cameron striding around Brussels thinking he's cock of the walk when everyone else just thinks he's a dick. His much-vaunted veto came to naught, leading that irrepressible wag Dennis Skinner to quip that had the PM just returned from Munich he would have been waving a piece of paper.

Then we had the hysterical headlines regarding William Hague leading a "mission" to Somalia. This had the effect of conjuring up the image of Hague as a gun-toting diminutive Yorkshire Rambo—or a shrivelled Ross Kemp—rather than the usual imperialist posturing. As if that wasn't enough we have a British warship, HMS Dauntless, steaming towards the Malvinas in a ludicrous display of literal gunboat diplomacy.

It is telling that all those media outlets who are falling over themselves to be seen as the most jingoistic tub-thumpers for this blatant act of aggression and whip their readers into a Thatcherite frenzy over the seemingly impending orgy of violence are curiously vague about the exact geographical location of the islands.

Perhaps because even the most slope-browed, knuckle-dragging Sun reader would take one look at a map and think: "Hang on a minute! They're about as British as Lionel Messi."

The way the red-tops are banging on about it you'd think they were located just off the Isle of Wight and bands of swarthy Latin Americans were at this moment rowing towards Portsmouth under a skull and crossbones. Daily Mail readers are probably shooting their daughters just to be safe.

But of course you cannot truly address the issue of denial without mentioning the Lib Dems. Energy Secretary Chris Huhne emerged yesterday from home to say he was resigning to spend more time with his constituents and fight the charge of perverting the course of justice—a phrase more usually associated with the Lib Dems' coalition colleagues—over allegations he got his (now) ex-wife to accept penalty points on his behalf.

Huhne of course declared his innocence, and who are we to say otherwise? But … it would be tempting to say that if, as is alleged—and only alleged of course—you had done such a thing it might not then be a good idea to have an affair and become embroiled in an acrimonious divorce with that individual … just a thought.

But the Gold Cup for self-deception must go to another Lib Dem this week.

Yes, Tory lackey and all-round lickspittle Nick Clegg—remember him?—once more demonstrated that straight-shooting honesty for which he is so esteemed in his constituency of Sheffield Hallam.

It's not often you will find this column supporting the House of Lords, but...

With breathtaking arrogance Clegg rounded on the Lords yesterday for being out of touch with the public for repeatedly blocking the government's attempts to destroy the lives of millions with its savage welfare cuts. This is probably the only example in living memory of the peers having their fingers on the pulse.

He then went on to say that the Lords were "irrelevant"— a dangerous word to bandy around for the leader of a party which couldn't get elected if there was only one name on the ballot and Paddy Ashdown herded voters to the polls with a Chieftain tank.

s right to kill up
"really honestly" believed

Hara-kiri on

With two
months to
go until
the general
election both
Labour and the
Tories were doing
their best 'After
you'/'No, after
YOU' routine with
a string
of gaffes
ranging
from Lord
Ashcroft's
dodgy donations to
David Miliband's
enthusiastic
support for torture

Cameron's dithering deals a blow to party electoral fortunes

Tories on the run as polls lead crumbles

CONSERVATIVE DONATIONS

Tory boss refuses to repay Ashcroft cash

Cameron tries to draw line under wealthy non-dom donor affair

Government produces last-minute evidence on Diego Garcia rendition ~ then demands secret hearing to hide the truth

YET ANOTHER TORTURE COVER-UP

nting the possibili
and confess all, re
devote the rest of

"adviser" to JP Mo
s after he handed b

absolutely everyo

ssianic tendencies

g at his blatant h
d by the breathtak

tember 11 to the

ght years ago.

this egregious c

D o any of the major parties actually want to win this election? I only ask because Labour and the Tories seem to be engaged in their own private version of mutually assured destruction.

Polls are notoriously inaccurate so should not be heeded too closely, like the drunk guy at the bar who tells you to put your house on a three-legged donkey in the 2.30 at Aintree.

The Daily Mail could probably conjure up a survey which showed that 99 per cent of British people wanted to bring back hanging for foxes.

But the Tories seem to believe the polls … and then panic if it looks like they're doing too well.

Every time it appears they've put clear blue water between themselves and Labour, they contrive to commit political hara-kiri in the spectacular manner of a samurai who's just discovered the Black & Decker hedge trimmer. Not that I'm complaining, mind you. The whole debacle has been hugely entertaining.

First we had the apparently numerically dyslexic shadow chancellor who wouldn't know a decimal point from a beauty spot and whose shadow budget was billions out in its sums.

It takes a certain amount of flair to be so ludicrously wrong all the time and still not actually admit you're an idiot.

This is the man who is perilously close to getting his hands on all our money and I wouldn't trust him with a child's piggy bank. It's as if he was living in a parallel universe—the Cameron Zone, where balls-ups become triumphs and you harvest the rewards for incompetence. Maybe he should consider a job at RBS?

Then, as if these golden gaffes were not enough, we had the glorious idiocy of the "We can't go on like this" election posters which somehow managed to make David Cameron look even more like a giant parboiled baby than he does in real life.

There have been suggestions that the posters were airbrushed, but I'm not so sure—he really is that smug.

Then, when the tears of laughter from the general public had almost dried, the Tories blundered head first into the Ashcroft scandal.

Lord Ashcroft has by his own estimation funnelled over £10 million into the Tories' coffers. But they claim they only just found out he wasn't paying taxes here.

Two possibilities immediately spring to mind—either they're lying or they're incompetent. Neither are particularly enticing qualities in a prospective government.

In fact, with such a disastrous campaign, the only reason they're still in the running is that Labour is now so punch-drunk that it can't even take proper advantage.

Labour is so mired in allegations of torture, deception and illegal warmongering that it's not a case of being unable to see the wood for the trees but rather not being able to see the effluent for the moral sewer into which it has sunk.

David Miliband can't seem to make his mind up as to whether he's happier denying that he tortured Muslims or cosying up to Israel and the US—not that the two are mutually exclusive. As for the rest of the Cabinet, they seem to have disappeared up their own fundaments.

The allegations of Gordon Brown's temper tantrums last week have failed to have the damaging effect that his political enemies would have hoped for, mainly because his stock with the public has fallen so low that it actually makes him seem slightly more interesting and human.

Bullying is nothing to joke about, but the evidence of such a claim doesn't really seem to stand up. Brown is alleged to have shouted at a few people after they made monumental cock-ups and punched a car seat in frustration. Sounds like an average night out for a lot of people.

One thing however is clear—his envy and anger towards Tony Blair. Brown was probably secretly seething that he didn't get as many protesters as his former boss at his Chilcot appearance. You can just imagine him roaring at his aides: "Why does Tony always get all the publicity? I've killed people too you know!"

as right to kill up †
"really honestly" believe

Nanny state

lay
cha
r s
rtm

fel
hir
be

is r
ici

eek
th
p
b
b

was

hose
not
on

thir

icul

decided to rule ou†
r's smugness and me:
ausing a conflagrat:
ng act of self-immo

nting the possibili
and confess all, re
devote the rest of

"adviser" to JP Mo:
s after he handed b:

he stand at an inqu
he Hague, he took a
d Lansdowne Partner

ssianic tendencies

g at his blatant h
d by the breathtak

tember 11 to the l

ght years ago.

this egregious c

One of the first acts by the coalition of millionaires was to refuse to sign an international treaty protecting domestic workers-- presumably for fear they'd be banned from beating the hired help

EMPLOYMENT

Britain bails out of domestic worker treaty

Anti-slavery activists attack government's 'cowardly stance' on private labour issue

You almost have to admire the sheer gall of this coalition, particularly the Tories—they always have another trick up their sleeve to blindside you with.

Much in the manner of smarmy magician David Copperfield they employ sleight of hand by doing something so breathtakingly cynical in plain sight that the public think: "Well, they couldn't possibly top that."

And then they do, behind the curtain, with the complicity of their less than lovely assistants Nick Clegg and Vince Cable.

Doing their level best to eradicate safety at work, put thousands of lives at risk, destroy the NHS and force the disabled back into work is the equivalent of pulling a mangy rabbit from a hat.

This week, however, they went for the big show-stopping number and decided to do their bit to perpetuate slavery. This is ironic on a number of levels, not least because the finale of most magic shows involves someone *escaping* from chains.

But not with this government and its Cabinet of mendacity. It's more like the old favourite, death by a thousand cuts. The UN International Labour Organisation's domestic worker convention would have enshrined in international law protections for those forced into Dickensian-style servitude in Britain. In particular it would have allowed for inspections of properties to ensure that no abuse of domestic staff occurs, something the Tories were very keen not to agree with for some reason.

The fact that the majority of the Cabinet are stinking-rich aristos reared by nannies—and whose own offspring probably recognise the hired help before they do mater and pater—has absolutely nothing to do with this decision of course.

Likewise, the fact that a large proportion of their core voters probably see nothing wrong with people being trafficked into indentured servitude, beaten and abused by their rich employers—as long as they're foreigners of course—is entirely coincidental.

The ILO treaty, as you would hope in 2011, has received almost universal backing except—quelle surprise—from GB plc. Silly me, I thought they were AGAINST the nanny state!

To the outrage of unions and campaigners, Britain opted out and abstained on the vote, claiming it already provided "comprehensive protections to domestic workers" and did not "consider it appropriate or practical" to extend those provisions.

"However, we do strongly support the principles the ILO treaty enshrines."

Oh really? Well that's all right then, as long as you support it in principle. It's not like they're real people or anything is it? That's like saying you agree with the abolition of the death penalty in principle while refusing to ban the shipping of execution drugs to the US until the courts tell you to … oh.

Principle is a very elastic concept for David Cameron and his chums who are gleefully waging war in Libya to, ahem, "protect the human rights of the Libyan people" but won't sign a treaty which would enshrine the rights of millions.

It's like abolition never happened, which in a very real sense it didn't for thousands of people in this country.

If the Tories' current private member's Bill to undermine the minimum wage goes through there will be thousands more toiling for a pittance and now they've wrecked the pension system they'll have to do it for life.

William Wilberforce and Thomas Clarkson would be rotating in their graves. They'll be bringing back child labour next. And rickets.

"Got too many kids you dole-scrounging scum? Get 'em up the chimney. Put 'em down the pit. Oh, haven't we got any of those any more?" They'll probably call it something like the "not-so-big society" or "Little Britain."

We're all in this together unless you're poor, foreign or both—in which case you're on your own.

s right to kill up 1
"really honestly" believeu

A shameless

The Victim Support
charity revealed
that an unrepentant
burglar,
forced to
write to
his victims
in Leeds
under the
'restorative
justice' scheme,
had called them
'thick' and said
the burglary was
their own fault.
The charity didn't
name the culprit
but the Star got
hold of an
exclusive

CRIME

Burglar mocks 'stupid' victims

Victim Support calls abusive letter a disgrace

decided to rule ou1
r's smugness and mei
ausing a conflagrat:
ng act of self-immo

ting the possibili

s after he handed ba

e stand at an inqu
e Hague, he took a
d Lansdowne Partner

absolutely everyor

ssianic tendencies

g at his blatant h
d by the breathtak

tember 11 to the 1

ight years ago.

this egregious c

probably really ho...tly ...lieved he was right to ...n't ... they

trigger some form of chain reaction cau... ...gratio ...t and therefore an unwitting act of self-immola

crook writes

A leading charity hit out this week at a callous letter written to a victim of crime under the restorative justice scheme from a recalcitrant thief who looted their home and personal belongings.

The letter written by a semi-literate felon under instruction from the Ministry of Justice branded the family from Leeds as "stupid" and said he had no sympathy or remorse as it was their own fault.

At no small expense or effort this column has managed to obtain an exclusive glimpse of the offending document.

It is believed to have been written by a serial offender in his forties thought to operate in the Westminster area and appearing utterly without shame in regard to his campaign of crime and we will now publish it in full to name and shame the verminous varlet involved.

Dear Victim,

I do not know why I am bothering to write to you. I have been forced to write this letter by the government.

I am not sorry for the fact that I burgled your country. Basically it was your fault anyway.

I am going to run you through the dumb mistakes you made.

Firstly, you left your 'X' in a box marked Conservative on May 10 which most people know not to do before they go to sleep.

Secondly, you are dumb because you are a peasant and live in the north which everyone knows is a high-risk area with people like me about.

Thirdly, you left your hard-earned savings in a bank and then made me Chancellor which I wouldn't do in a million years.

But anyway I don't feel sorry for you and I'm not going to give you any sympathy or show any remorse.

Yours Sincerely
Gideon Osborne

When presented with a copy of said epistle a source at the Metropolitan Police said: "This is a particularly sick individual who we've had our eye on for some time. We would urge members not to approach this individual who is clearly delusional and a serious danger to society. We welcome the publication of the letter as a warning for people to secure their homes and their pensions by ensuring they do not vote Tory again."

He continued: "Between you and me we'd like to give him a good kicking down the cells but we just haven't got the staff these days and anyway Theresa May is at the top of the list and we have to wait for the Border Agency to finish first."

In fact so short-staffed are the Met in these straitened times that they were forced yet again this week to resort to drafting in occasional special constable Boris Johnson on a series of dawn raids across the metropolis.

Surely that amounts to cruel and unusual punishment? Not only do you get your door booted down by the Sweeney but you have to suffer a bumbling oaf mumbling: "Don't mind me! Are you Turkish by any chance? I say, my great grandfather was Turkish, Ottoman Empire and all that, quite unfortunate how it all turned out really...

"And what do you do? Drug dealer eh? Marvellous! Shows good entrepreneurial spirit. Well, anyway, keep up the good work. Er, cripes! No, gosh, bit of a gaffe there but think I got away with it. Not like you eh chappy? Ha! Ha!

"Ah, cocaine, don't mind if I do, I tried the old nose candy once with the Bully Club but I sneezed ... er, have you got a £50 note at all? I usually got one from Osborne."

as right to kill up †
"really honestly" believeu

Secret diary

The Tories may have stuck doggedly to the 'No money left' line but someone evidently forgot to copy Michael Gove into the memo as the rubber-faced man/boy complained that not enough was being spent on the jubilee and proposed smoothing Her Majesty's ruffled feelings by buying her a new £60m yacht

decided to rule out
r's smugness and mer
ausing a conflagrat:
ng act of self-immo

nting the possibili
and confess all, re
devote the rest of

"adviser" to JP Mo:
s after he handed ba

he stand at an inqu
he Hague, he took a
d Lansdowne Partner

absolutely everyor

DIAMOND JUBILEE
Gove floats new royal yacht 'present'

THE Tories say they have declared war on "state scroungers," but that didn't stop Michael Grove suggesting yesterday that taxpayers should buy royal sponsers a new yacht to mark the Queen's Diamond Jubilee.

The Education Secretary, who has presided over multi million-pound cuts to schools, complained over not enough had been spent on celebrating the royal occasion.

In a leaked letter to fellow ministers Mr Gove said a "fitting" way to mark the jubilee would be "a gift from the nation to her majesty...a royal yacht."

Labour said the idea demonstrated Mr Gove was [...] of touch" to think such expenditure was appro-

priate at a time of massive cuts.

The party deputy chairman Tom Watson said: "When school budgets are being slashed, parents will be wondering how Gove came even to suggest this idea.

"This is not the time to spend £60 million on a yacht."

Prime Minister David Cameron was forced yesterday to publicly rule the idea "inappropriate" in a time of economic austerity.

Mr Gove denied suggesting taxpayers' money should be used to buy the yacht, insisting he was referring to a new boat as part of the Future Ship Project — a donation-funded plan to give "disadvantaged youth" the chance "to learn new skill[...]

FLAG SHIP: Former Royal Yacht

tember 11 to the 1

ight years ago.

this egregious c

January 1 2012—Dear Diary, got an action man for Christmas and a Beano annual. When will Mum realise that I'm almost a grown-up and an intellectual? But they have given me a brilliant new idea for revitalising the education system, cutting the armed forces budget and saving society in one go.

Send the troublemaking oiks to boot camp to put some discipline into them—I wish they'd had that in my day. Maybe it would have stopped Eric Pickles stealing my dinner money.

Squeezed zits, then measured my thing while thinking of the blessed Maggie.

January 6—Got strong support for my boot camp proposal from Dave and even the Lib Dems are keen on it. I like having them around because it makes me look less wimpy.

Painted room black to to reflect the agony in my soul (and to cover up Star Wars wallpaper).

My thing has shrunk.

January 10—This year will mark the 60th anniversary of the ascension of Her Majesty Queen Elizabeth II to the throne. Got out bunting from last year's royal wedding, blew off the dust and festooned the house.

Dad said I was mental and anyway we're Scottish. Reminded him the royal consort is called the Duke of Edinburgh!

Took bunting down again and hid with special magazine under bed. Hope this is not disrespectful.

January 13—Friday the 13th! Eric Pickles asked me if I'd ever seen blue goldfish. Said everyone knows goldfish are orange! Had head flushed down toilet.

January 16—Had another brilliant idea, while in the bath! Now I know how Archimedes felt.

Wrote to Dave on my new special notepaper and suggested we buy a royal yacht to mark Her Majesty's jubilee. He sounded quite keen on the idea but didn't like my drawing—or the suggestion it be red, white and blue. It's not easy being an intellectual.

January 17—Someone leaked my letter to Dave (I bet it was one of those Lib Dems, or Pickles!) Had to deny I suggested buying a yacht with taxpayers' money as apparently things are quite tight at the moment.

Decided to eke out my Christmas chocolate because if things carry on like this we'll have to bring rationing back.

Yes, that's right, the country is going to the dogs, there is civil unrest on the streets, an unelected government is driving through brutal austerity cuts and letting its chums in big business get away with murder.

And what is the coalition's solution to the myriad ills they have inflicted on our society? Let's all club together and buy the royals a boat.

According to a leaked letter this week weird man/boy Michael Gove thinks that the panacea for all our woes is to blow £60 million on said yacht for the Windsors to mark the diamond jubilee. First they tell us we all have to tighten our belts and watch our pay being frozen or in fact cut and then they try and sneak through plans for a state funeral for Thatcher and then propose we also shell out for a new boat for those freeloaders in Buck House.

The missive from Gove stated: "My suggestion would be a gift from the nation to the Queen thinking about, for example, David Willetts's excellent suggestion for a royal yacht—and something tangible to commemorate this momentous occasion."

Gove was then forced to distance himself from the letter with his lackeys at the Department of Education describing it as "loosely worded."

Well, this is the same man who made 25 errors in his first policy document, so it would be true to form.

Personally this column would like to propose that demanding a gift TO the nation FROM those spoilt spongers for having kept them in the lap of luxury for 60 bloody years would be more appropriate.

A mass abdication should just about do it.

s right to kill up 1
"really honestly" believe

Let down by

lay
cha
r s
rtm

fel
hir
be

is I
ici

eek
th
pop
ks

bab
lf.

was

hose
not
on

thi

icul

decided to rule ou1
r's smugness and mer
ausing a conflagrat:
ng act of ... immo

Didn't the Tories once have a reputation for razor-sharp repartee? Winston Churchill would be spinning in his grave at the antics of today's rightwingers as Jeremy Clarkson followed David Cameron's 'Calm down, dear' and George Osborne's 'pantomime dame' dig with an oh-so-hilarious call for striking public servants to be shot in front of their families

MILLIONAIRE BIGMOUTH
BBC urged to fire Cameron's chum Clarkson after 'shoot the workers' rant

he Hague, he took a
d Lansdowne Partner

absolutely everyor

ssianic tendencies

g at his blatant h
d by the breathtak

tember 11 to the 1

ght years ago.

this egregious c

...probably really he...ly believed he was right to... ...they...

the putdowns

trigger some form of chain reaction cau... ...gratio ...and therefore an unwitting act of self-immola

You just don't get the same calibre of right-wing reactionary bigots these days, do you? Where is the panache, the savoir faire, the rapier-like badinage of yesteryear?

Say what you want about Churchill—and he was a vicious old sod—but he had a way with a putdown. By comparison the current crop are smirking simpletons and bellowing buffoons who wouldn't know a mot juste from a Moët & Chandon.

PM's questions and Commons debates used to be conducted amid a flurry of cutting barbs and razor-sharp ripostes but have now sunk to sub-playground name-calling and pathetic hand gestures.

When nicking a line from Michael Winner (David Cameron) or making a homophobic dig (George Osborne) is the best gag you can come up with, it's a pretty pathetic state of affairs.

And the Labour double act of the Two Eds is no better. They may think they are as acerbically urbane as Statler and Waldorf.

But with their choreographed waving like the world's worst boy band as they attempt to deride the Tories, they more accurately resemble those other Jim Henson creations—Sesame Street's Ernie and Bert.

To return to the events of recent days, the main problem with the posturing Tory politicos is that they do not comprehend the first rule of comedy and satire.

Like a grappling hook or—to put it into terms they might comprehend—social climbing, it only works when directed upwards.

Sneering at those less fortunate than yourself or tossing out lazy racial slurs does not constitute wit. It's boorish bullying.

They can't even stick to a consistent line. In the run-up to November 30 the Tories went from mocking the unions to howling like banshees with Tourette's that the strike would wreck the country and drive us all into penury and pauperdom.

Presumably they were irked because that's their role and they've been doing a bloody good job of it up to now.

Then, when two million people took to the streets to vent their disgust at the draconian cuts, the self-same doommongers tried to claim it was a mere trifle.

Cameron blustered that the biggest show of trade union strength in a generation had been "a damp squib." It's that sort of arrogant denial and wilful distortion of the facts that only comes with a career in politics preceded by a previous job in PR.

The rest of his cronies did their best to abuse and insult those on strike, only stopping short of going down to the picket lines and waving wodges of fivers at them while singing My Old Man's A Dustman in a mock cockney accent.

All of which brings us neatly to professional bigot and self-publicist Jeremy Clarkson.

His predictably crass comment on the One Show, that striking public-sector workers should be executed in front of their families, caused outrage among unions and a large section of the public. Which was exactly what it was intended to do. The hypocrisy of a vastly wealthy TV "personality" spouting off about the public-sector workers striking to "protect their gold-plated pensions" while others, such as he, "have to work for a living" was lost on no-one, especially him.

I call him a professional bigot because he does it for money and is paid staggeringly well for doing so.

By a strange coincidence, his most deliberately obnoxious comments always tend to coincide with the publication of his latest book or DVD, as they did this time. Clarkson is the equivalent of the school bully who only ever picks on the afflicted or those he deems inferior—or at least pretends to.

While Clarkson is a professional offence-giver, there is one veteran gifted amateur who has been ploughing a lone furrow for years.

This week, however, the Duke of Edinburgh unaccountably took his eye off the ball when faced with what you would have thought for him would have been the opportunity of a lifetime.

Quite who decided it would be a good idea to put a racist shooting fanatic in the same room as Yoko Ono, we may never know...

is right to kill up 1
"really honestly" believed

Gallery of

David Cameron's
first Cabinet
reshuffle left many
asking what it
would take to get
sacked as disgraced
David Laws, bigot
Chris Grayling and
Murdoch lickspittle
Jeremy Hunt all
landed plum roles
in a government of
no talents at all

lay
cha
f s
rtm

fel
hir
be

is r
ici

eek
th
pop
ks

bab
lf.

vas

hose
not
on

thi

icul

decided to rule out
r's smugness and mer
ausing a conflagrat
ng act of self-immo

nting the possibili
and confess all, re
devote the rest of

"adviser" to JP Mo
s after he handed b

ne stand at an inqu
ne Hague, he took a
d Lansdowne Partner

ly everyor

es

h
tak

e]

this egregious c

MINISTER OF NO JOB: Ken Clarke

OUT TO DESTROY NHS: Jeremy Hunt

OFF YOU GO: George Young

CAMERON RESHUFFLES HIS PACK OF WOLVES

PM shoves government further to right with new line-up

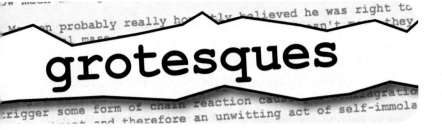

grotesques

"I say George, things are looking a bit sticky for us at the moment. People really seem to hate us despite all our wonderful ideas."

"I know Dave, who'd have thought the proles would get so uppity over a few teensy cuts and the odd missing decimal point?"

"Well you did make a complete pig's arse of the Budget, just like when it was your turn to buy the plonk in the Bully Club, what!"

"I have nightmares about villagers coming for us with pitchforks and burning torches."

"Don't be silly, after what we've done to the economy they won't be able to afford the petrol."

"They will—Maude told them to stockpile it, remember?"

"Oh God, why am I surrounded by incompetents?"

"You've still got me Dave."

"That's rather my point Gideon. We have to do something. I don't suppose..."

"Why are you looking at me like that Dave? I'm not doing the honourable thing, it's not in my character, and anyway that's what we've got the Lib Dems for."

"I fear it might be too late for that. There's only one thing for it—we've got to stuff the Cabinet with a load of people even more hated than us! Where's Grayling? He's a prize bastard."

"Yes, yes, compared to him people would see us for who we really are."

"God no, we don't want that!"

As desperate last throws of the dice go David Cameron's reshuffle was not so much rearranging the foldable seating on an infamously porous vessel as fiddling the books while Rome burns.

A gruesome gallery of grotesques were wheeled out squinting into the searing light of day like Nosferatu on a Club 18-30 holiday. In Jeremy Hunt and George Osborne's cases no doubt amazed they had dodged a bullet or at least a judiciously placed stake.

There were reports of tears and snotters around Downing Street but then Ken Clarke had probably had a few before he went in.

As statements of intent go this was Cameron saying that, not content with just being the nasty party any more, he was going to up the ante and turn it into the total vicious bastard party.

This, it was claimed, was a Cabinet that "meant business." More like a Cabinet which means business can do whatever the hell it wants.

There were new appointments for Minister for Murdoch Jeremy Hunt and Chris Grayling, and David Laws is back in the Cabinet having had to quit over a taxpayer-funded attempt to stay in the closet. What does it take to get sacked from this government? Like the banking industry it worships so much, it would appear that total incompetence need not be a bar to promotion with the Con-Dems.

Hunt was parachuted into the health brief even after becoming as toxic as an FSB teapot after his blatant toadying to the dark side over the BSkyB bid and his bizarre text messages to News Corp lobbyist Fred Michel.

Hunt is an ideal candidate to run the health service—into the ground. As Culture Secretary he even attempted to cut the NHS scenes from the Olympic opening ceremony.

And he's a well-known advocate for homeopathy. I think we have some idea of what's in store—a massively watered-down NHS which can only provide the notion of being beneficial.

And then there was Grayling...

Appointing the rabid rightwinger, his hands still dripping with the blood of workers due to his frenzied slashing of health and safety regulations, as Justice Secretary is like making Jack the Ripper a High Court judge.

It was Grayling, you will recall, who famously defended the right of a pair of Christian bigots to discriminate against gay couples and ban them from sharing a room in their B&B.

And just to add to the fun Cameron appointed an Environment Minister—Owen Paterson—who is a climate-change denier and an Equalities Secretary, Maria Miller, who opposes equality.

The only real surprise was that Aidan Burley wasn't appointed Defence Secretary—he's already got a uniform.

as right to kill up 1
"really honestly" believe

Coup,

decided to rule ou1
r's smugness and mer
ausing a conflagrat:
ng act of self-immo

nting the possibili
and confess all, re
devote the rest of

Simon Mann, the mercenary 'mastermind' and ex-SAS officer, flew home after serving just 15 months for a bungled putsch in Equatorial Guinea by a team of hired killers straight out of Some Mothers Do 'Ave 'Em

EQUATORIAL GUINEA
Full pardon given to coup plot members

BRITISH coup-plotter Simon Mann and four South African mercenaries were flown home yesterday after being pardoned for plotting to overthrow the government of Equatorial Guinea.

g at his blatant h
d by the breathtak

tember 11 to the

ght years ago.

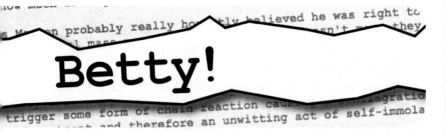

Betty!

It was supposed to be Wild Geese but it played out more like Some Mothers Do 'Ave 'Em. Yes, that's right, this week saw the release of old Etonian gun-for-hire Simon Mann, mastermind—and I use the term in its loosest sense—of the 2004 "wonga" coup in Equatorial Guinea.

Mann was freed from his Black Beach gulag having served a gruelling 15 months of his 34-year sentence. I've heard of time off for good behaviour, but this is ridiculous.

Though for once the penal system does appear to have had a rehabilitative effect. Mann emerged blinking into the daylight and immediately pledged to shop all his co-conspirators to the authorities. There's no honour among thieves, as the old adage goes, and that apparently goes double for blood-soaked mercenaries banged up in chokey.

Hell hath no fury like a hired killer scorned—or one who's just found out that the cheque bounced.

It seems like only yesterday that a rag-tag team of around 70 "crack" mercenaries were hauled from a plane in Zimbabwe during one of the most ill-advised stop-offs since Roman Polanski got a craving for Toblerone.

Less the A-Team than the under-21 third-string reserves, these bold warriors were thwarted in their noble mission to line their pockets and made to look, well, a bit pathetic really. But then what can you expect when you look at the calibre of some of those involved in the attempted coup?

Mann himself was a former officer in the SAS before leaving for more lucrative pastures and teaming up with Tim Spicer in Sandline International.

Remember them? The Korporate Killers cut a bloody swathe through Papua New Guinea, Sierra Leone and Angola, propping up corrupt regimes with one lascivious eye on their conflict-diamond profits.

Tellingly, one of the claims made by Mann in his attempts to worm his way out of trouble this time round was that the planned coup had actually just been a security operation for mining interests in the region. If in doubt rely on the old fall-back, eh?

For someone with such a repugnant yet successful track record it is all the more surprising who Mann decided would make an ideal partner in the coup.

When most people think of Mark "are we there yet?" Thatcher, they do not automatically think of a member of a well-oiled paramilitary-style organisation. You wouldn't let him read the map for a start.

But apparently old Etonian ties run deep. Either that or—probably more likely—if you are casting around for an idiot with a disposable income, a monstrous ego and an unquench-able greed...

It would be uncharitable, if accurate, to say that from this point on the mission was, to quote Private Frazer, "doomed."

Thatcher—or "Scratcher," as he was ingeniously code-named—shelled out about a quarter of a million dollars for a helicopter claiming he thought it was for an "air ambulance."

This, given his family's track record when it comes to sup-porting the health service, is about as credible as his mother saying that she was just worried the miners would get a nasty cough if she kept the pits open.

Employing his one true talent, Thatcher managed to weasel his way out of a hefty prison sentence in South Africa by copping a plea bargain and hightailing it to Spain.

Mann's disclosures regarding the role not just of Thatcher but the alleged part played by oil tycoon Eli Calil in the plot will make fascinating reading.

With friends like these, who needs enemas.

as right to kill up
"really honestly" believe

The Tories'

There's a chronic
housing shortage,
homelessness is
rampant, and rents
and house prices
are rocketing.
How to tackle
the crisis? Ban
people from
occupying
empty
buildings,
of course.
If we're thinking
about outlawing
anti-social
parasites there are
better places to
start...

decided to rule out
r's smugness and me
ausing a conflagrat
ng act of self-immo

nting the possibili
and confess all, re
devote the rest of

"adviser" to JP Mo
after he handed b

HOUSING
**Total squatting ban
comes into force**

ok a
d Lansdowne Partner

absolutely everyo

ssianic tendencies

g at his blatant h
d by the breathtak

tember 11 to the

ight years ago.

this egregious c

squat thrust

This week there has been much debate over plans to end an anti-social activity which has been the bane of civilised society and strikes fear into the hearts of homeowners everywhere.

This parasitic practice has been going on for far too long and it is time to stamp it out with the utmost vigour.

Public and private properties are wrested from their rightful owners and run into the ground. The offenders cause a public nuisance, pay no rent on their temporary dwellings and contribute nothing to society.

Let's outlaw the Tory Party now. Housing Minister Grant Shapps yesterday rolled out plans to make the squatting of vacant residential properties illegal, meaning anyone found guilty could face six months in prison, a £5,000 fine or both.

He said: "For too long, hard-working people have faced long legal battles to get their homes back from squatters, and repair bills reaching into the thousands when they finally leave."

That sentence works equally well if you change the word "homes" for "public services," "squatters" for "Tories" and "thousands" for "billions."

Meanwhile, Justice Minister Crispin Blunt said: "For too long, squatters have had the justice system on the run and have caused homeowners untold misery in eviction, repair and clean-up costs. Hard-working homeowners need and deserve a justice system where their rights come first."

This from a government which is hell-bent on forcing through secret trials to prevent its complicity in the rendition and torture of its own citizens coming out, a government which is systematically attempting to tear up centuries of British legal tradition, scrap habeas corpus and place itself and its minions in the secret service above the law.

This is also the same bunch who broke their promise to end child detention and continue to bang up innocent kids in appalling conditions. It would appear these unfortunate minors don't need or deserve a justice system where their rights come first.

Even ignoring all the moral arguments against the policy, it doesn't make economic sense. Allowing people to occupy vacant properties costs the government nothing. Banging someone up for six months costs an estimated £20,000.

This is a coalition that has moved into Downing Street without being invited, wrecked the country, vandalised the economy, thumbed its nose at the law and trashed its public pledges. Sounds rather like their definition of squatting doesn't it?

By contrast, although not all squatters are saints, many do up dilapidated buildings which otherwise would fall further into ruin, start up community projects and cause little or no trouble to the surrounding community. I know who I'd rather have as neighbours.

At a time when the government is slashing housing benefit, refusing to crack down on unscrupulous landlords jacking up rents sky high and forcing thousands out of work, it is now attempting to make thousands more homeless.

And while we're on the subject of rank hypocrisy, this column seems to recall that it wasn't so long ago that quite a number of these self-same politicians were in a bit of hot water for flipping their second homes and defrauding the taxpayer with their expenses claims.

That, however, was deemed not to be illegal in the majority of cases.

Talk about a culture of entitlement. If the government had any moral scruples at all it would make it illegal for the wealthy to own multiple homes, many of which are left empty for the majority of the year, issue compulsory seizure orders on landed estates and convert them into affordable public housing.

The Windsors have got a few we could start with. Then there's Chequers. Now why would the Cabinet of millionaires and aristos not think that was a good idea?

Gold in the

Team GB raked in the Olympic medals thanks to one athlete who'd be sent to Somalia if the Tories had their way and others whose careers were born on playing fields that are being dug up and flogged to Tesco. But that didn't stop Cameron and co covering themselves in other people's glory

OLYMPICS: HISTORIC MOMENT FOR BRITISH SPORT

The proudest day
Triumphant athletes revel in sensational results

HE'S DONE IT!
Wiggins rides into record books: p16

decided to rule ou
r's smugness and me
ausing a conflagrat
ng act of self-immo

s right to kill up
"really honestly" believe

at his blatant h
d by the breathtak

tember 11 to the

ght years ago.

this egregious c

glory hunt

And the gold medal in the freestyle bandwagon jump goes to ... the Conservative Party! When what should be being heralded is the supreme athleticism of the participants at the Games, regardless of nationality, the Tories have used it as a giant schmoozefest-stroke-propaganda-exercise.

The sheer quantity of jingoistic garbage being spewed forth in recent months has reached nauseating proportions of late.

And of course David Cameron et al are at the head of the field when it comes to coating themselves in someone else's glory. The way they've been banging on you'd think it was them who'd won the medals.

When you consider that the Tories did everything in their power to cock up this Olympics, from ethically abhorrent sponsorship deals with sweatshop exploiters and planet rapers to handing the security contract to the private sector's equivalent of Laurel and Hardy, it's a bit rich to see their smirking faces claiming ill-deserved plaudits.

We've had Cameron strutting around like a puffed-up peacock bragging about Britain's success, making much use of the collective "we" and making snide digs at foreigners.

In an interview on Thursday with that infamously hard-hitting interrogator Chris Evans he said: "We've got a system that seems to be delivering. It's driving the French mad." Which is one step away from "Take that Johnny frog leg" and "They don't like it up 'em."

He then made reference to the Tour de France, adding: "All those Union Jacks on the Champs-Élysées must have been a bit hard to take." Personally I'm finding all those Union Jacks in Hackney a bit hard to take.

The achievement of Britain's athletes has been phenomenal but you'd think we were the only country involved from the Beeb's legendarily, ahem … unpartisan coverage.

Indeed the level of blinkered patriotism reached its apogee this week with crowds of braying imbeciles turning out in their droves to rah-rah a bunch of pampered ponces on prancing horses.

Oh, they can call it dressage all they want but that is not a sport. We were treated to the sight of a rather plummy type attempting to claim that it was not an elitist event. "Anyone can take part," he blathered. Yeah, if you have a horse. Which, let's face it, tends to exclude all but the chattering classes. Not many council estates have paddocks these days.

"We have got a great system so let's build on that and then when we go to Rio in 2016 we can have a good experience," Cameron further chuntered.

We? Funny I don't recall seeing him busting a gut and training for four years to get a medal. He had 13 years to get in shape to run the country and look what happened there.

Not to be outdone we have also had blonde blunderer Boris Johnson waffling on about how the Olympics is a vindication of multicultural Britain and the Conservative view of life.

This would be the Conservatives whose leader recently went on an Enoch Powell-style rant about how multiculturalism had failed and whose immigration policies would have seen at least one British medal winner sent back to Somalia.

This would also be the Tory Party which scrapped free milk for schoolkids—it's probably quite difficult to run the 800 metres with rickets—is continuing to sell off school playing fields to anyone with enough cash and slashed sports funding.

It takes a spectacular degree of cynicism to tell us that the Olympics will inspire a new generation of athletes and at the same time make sure they have nowhere to practise unless they want to do the hurdles over shopping trolleys in the newly constructed Tesco car park.

Johnson then, inevitably, went on to contrast the Olympian spirit with that of last year's rioters.

It is interesting if unsurprising that the government is falling all over itself to claim credit for British athletes' success but anything they are responsible for—the economy, the NHS, social deprivation—is someone else's problem.

hearing I had reluctantly decided to rule
sheer enormity of Blair's smugness and me
form of chain reaction causing a conflagrati
and therefore an unwitting act of self-immo

did was try to link September 11 to the Ir
cular claim didn't hold water eight years a
evidence to support this egregious claim be

were carried out mainly by

urprise, surprise. Tony Blair thinks he wa
illion people in an illegal war because he
e was right.

ell, that was worth £250k of public money
nows how much in inquiry salaries, wasn't

arles Manson probably eally honestly beli
every egomani   derer in

Zealots

Blair was always going to allow his messi
—yet again.

as right to kill up
"really honestly" believed

Thou shalt

decided to rule out
r's smugness and me
ausing a conflagrat
ng act of self-immo

Tory peer Baroness Warsi got herself in hot water with the British Humanist Association after trying to paint the Catholic church (estimated wealth £200 billion) as the poor suffering victims during a brown-nosing visit to the Vatican, while the High Court slapped down Bideford Town Council's attempt to turn its meetings into prayer services

lay
cha
r s
rtm

fel
hir
be

is
ci

eek
th
pop
ks

bab
lf.

was

hose
not
on

thi

icul

RELIGION
BHA dismisses Warsi's 'outdated' views
Tory peer slammed for 'divisive' call

e stand at an inqu
e Hague, he took a
Lansdowne Partner

absolutely everyo

ssianic tendencies

g at his blatant h
d by the breathtak

RELIGION
Court to council: You don't have a prayer

Meanwhile

his egregious c

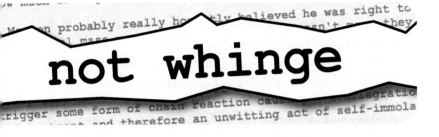

not whinge

Say what you want about the God squad, but when it comes to sanctimoniously taking the moral high ground, they're in a league of their own.

In recent days we have seen howls of outrage from various quarters over the claimed persecution of the Christian population in Britain.

It would appear that turning the other cheek is no longer in vogue.

On Tuesday we were greeted by the surreal sight of Tory chairwoman Baroness Warsi receiving a rapturous response from the Catholic hierarchy when she condemned the evils of "intolerant secularism" in this country.

It's not something you see every day—a Muslim female Tory MP giving a speech at the Vatican—but that's exactly what happened this week when the Yorkshire peer got up and addressed that famously tolerant body.

Of course she was—if you'll excuse the expression—somewhat preaching to the choir.

You're not exactly going to get heckled by the cardinals when your rallying call is for more religion in modern life. Even if you are a woman. Unsurprisingly it went down rather well.

To return to the central plank of her theory, that intolerant secularism is a blight on society, a few points if I may.

Since when has secularism been a threat to religion?

Since when has someone saying: "I'm not sure you're right about that, you know" been a bad thing?

When have you ever heard anyone declare a crusade or jihad in the name of theological uncertainty?

If you pick almost any instance of intolerance, bigotry, persecution and bloodshed throughout history the main candidates are invariably those who espouse some form of religious dogma, generally with them in the role of Messiah.

Historically of course one of the most infamous figures was a certain Torquemada...

And speaking of the Inquisition, Pope Benedict, or "God's Rottweiler" as he's affectionately known, was also for many years the head of that particular branch of religious zealots and they weren't exactly known for their tolerance of anything.

He has recent form too. In 2006 Il Papa got himself into a spot of hot water when he quoted a 14th-century Christian emperor who said Mohammed had brought the world only "evil and inhuman" things.

So not like those paragons of virtue in the Catholic church then ... who have brought the world nothing but sweetness and light—and a novel approach to child care.

The odious EDL also like to make out they're Christians, defending the true English faith from the barbarity of Islam. They're not of course. They are racist thugs.

Either that or they've taken a rather obscure interpretation of the parable about throwing the first stone.

Warsi called for faith to be given "a seat at the table" and more influence in politics. Well, that's never gone wrong has it?

To cite a few recent examples—Tony Blair, George Dubya Bush, the Ayatollah, Saudi Arabia and al-Qaida.

This patent claptrap coupled with the "woe is me-ing" of

Christian fundamentalists in recent days all adds up to a bizarre form of persecution complex.

This week we also had those enlightened people at Bideford Town Council wailing and gnashing their teeth after they were banned by the High Court from saying prayers before council meetings.

This, they claimed, was further evidence of the vicious persecution Christians face in this day and age.

Then we had the two bible-bashing B&B owners who claimed they were being picked on because they weren't allowed to discriminate against gay couples.

"How dare you not let me exercise my petty bigotries in the name of my imaginary friend of choice? It's political correctness gone mad!"

as right to kill up t
"really honestly" believe

World champs

It was a vintage
week for fools,
fraudsters and spin
doctors as Gordon
Brown's government
put a brave
face on soaring
joblessness,
Texas extremists
tried to shoehorn
God into school
textbooks and a
would-be nazi
bomber's own
lawyer rounded
on him

TERROR: Neil Lewington was
convicted of plotting bombings

POLITICAL EXTREMISM

Neonazi gets life for bomb plots against 'non-British'

Unemployment sees record rise

New Labour's worst jobless total
announced on day Jaguar axes
300 jobs at Merseyside factory

ght years ago.

probably really ho...tly believed he was right to ...they

# of delusion

trigger some form of chain reaction ca... ...agratio
...therefore an unwitting act of self-immola

I have been accused, probably quite rightly, of a fair degree of cynicism in my time, but still find myself dumbfounded by the spectacular attempts to spin the facts, mangle the truth and state the bleeding obvious made by our public representatives on an almost daily basis.

Take the last two weeks for example. We have had a government minister attempting to spin his way out of trouble over unemployment levels, saying that things would be much worse if the government hadn't intervened.

Given new Labour's recent record, that's akin to saying that the pensions deficit would have been much worse if Harold Shipman hadn't intervened.

The only way the government seems to have "intervened" at all was to bail out a bunch of avaricious yuppie scumbags in flash suits who, due to spectacular arrogance and total incompetence, are now down to their last Bentley.

Then this week we had a report published with much fanfare by a cross-party committee on equality headed by Alan "I'm working-class, me" Milburn.

As a result of exhaustive research, the committee reached the explosive conclusion that, er … quite a few judges and lawyers went to public school. Hold the front page!

Toffs more privileged shocker. What will their next earth-shattering revelation be? Royal family workshy idlers? Estate agents prone to terminological inexactitude? People who have open-heart surgery in hospital more likely to survive than those who use a Black and Decker Workmate?

And what radical plans does the committee propose to rectify this situation? The introduction of officer cadet corps in state schools, that's what. Well, that should certainly bring the ivory towers crumbling to the ground.

But when it comes to distortion and sheer self-delusion, you have to bow to the heavyweight champions of the world—the US religious right.

Not only did these people get a semi-literate war criminal installed as president twice and still manage to ignore the fact that he was perhaps the least plausible example of intelligent design in existence, they are now attempting literally to rewrite history.

In Texas, the state education board is considering a demand that children in schools be taught that there would be no United States without God.

A panel of "experts" tasked with "revising" the state's history includes a hellfire preacher who believes Hurricane Katrina and the ignominious defeat in Vietnam were God's way of punishing the US for its tolerance of homosexuality and several other fundamentalist Jesus creepers with views slightly to the right of Torquemada.

Well, that's all right then. As long as it's a balanced debate...

Religion did have a role to play in the formation of the US of course. The pilgrim fathers were so dementedly zealous that even the established churches said: "Hang on a minute, this is getting out of hand" and like a hyperactive child with ADHD sent them out to play in the brave new world.

Bizarrely, the only person who has been talking sense this week is a member of the legal profession. David Etherington QC, in the invidious position of defending neonazi wannabe bomber Neil Lewington and in an apparent stab at mitigation, described his client as a "silly, immature, alcoholic, dysfunctional twit, fantasising to make up for a rather sad life."

Nice to see that public-school education wasn't wasted.

s right to kill up
"really honestly" believe

The sins of

The Pope finally got around to saying sorry for decades of child abuse and cover-ups-- but the Catholic church swiftly ruined the good work by blaming the allegations on a conspiracy of journalists. Meanwhile, another serial criminal with a God complex lurched back into view in Sedgefield

decided to rule out
r's smugness and men
ausing a conflagrat

■ CATHOLIC CHURCH'S EASTER 'GUILT' OVER SEX ABUSE

he stand at an inqu
he Hague, he took a
d Lansdowne Partner

absolutely everyor

ELECTION
'No credibility'
Blair wheeled
out to support
Brown camp

tendencies

blatant h
e breathtak

FORMER Pri

11 to the 1

ars ago.

egregious c

ay
cha
r s
rtn

fel
hin
be

is
ici

eek
th
pop
ks

bab
lf

was

hose
not
on

thi

icul

the father

This being Easter and all, I thought it was high time this column turned its attention to the Catholic church and its peculiar take on pastoral care.

Allegations of child abuse within the church are nothing new, but the sheer cynicism of the organisation as allegations continue to emerge has taken many Catholics aback. And the allegations will continue, have no doubt of that.

Perverted priests who preyed on innocent children were an embarrassing inconvenience to the church hierarchy, which hushed it up and transferred paedophiles to new dioceses where they could once more abuse with impunity those they were supposed to be caring for.

When Jesus allegedly died for the sins of man, I can't help thinking this might not have been what he had in mind.

Any claim that the church was unaware of what was going on can be treated with the scorn it deserves. Bishops, cardinals and Pope Benedict himself, in his former incarnation as Prefect of the Congregation for the Doctrine of the Faith, have been involved in gagging children as young as eight and paying out hush money to avoid legal prosecutions.

The Congregation for the Doctrine is merely a modern term for the Inquisition and its role is defined as "to promote and safeguard the doctrine on the faith and morals throughout the Catholic world." That would, presumably, include pederast priests fiddling with small boys.

In 2009 the Irish Commission to Inquire into Child Abuse concluded that "the Dublin archdiocese's preoccupations in dealing with cases of child sexual abuse, at least until the mid-1990s, were the maintenance of secrecy, the avoidance of scandal, the protection of the reputation of the church and the preservation of its assets.

"All other considerations, including the welfare of children and justice for victims, were subordinated to these priorities."

And these are the people who presume to lecture us on morals? What did they think? That it was a mistranslation from the Latin—"Molest me father for I have sinned"?

In its usual up-front and honest way, the church and Il Papa himself issued an apology this week. But then, with the unseemly haste of a Donegal cleric in pursuit of an ice-cream van, it tried to turn the tables and say that the claims were a conspiracy whipped up by us verminous journos in the fourth estate to tarnish the good name of the church.

I dunno, one hack writer churns out a rubbish potboiler about murderous albino monks and Mary Magdalene and Jesus having a sprog and all of a sudden everything's a conspiracy.

Just for the record, the dictionary definition of conspiracy is as follows: "An evil, unlawful, treacherous or surreptitious plan formulated in secret by two or more persons; an agreement by two or more persons to commit a crime, fraud or other wrongful act." That sounds an awful lot like what the church has been doing for the last half-century and more. Let he who is without sin and all that…

Still, Easter is the time for repentance and forgiveness. Personally, I've always thought that giving up chocolate for a few weeks and then bingeing on Easter eggs was a bizarre way to worship. That's not religion, it's an eating disorder.

But in the spirit of the season, it is to be hoped that members of the church hierarchy will lead by example—and give up their jobs.

And, speaking of unrepentant Catholics who moved to another job to avoid prosecution, who should loom into view this week with a general election beckoning but Britain's own war criminal extraordinaire?

Yes, that's right. Tony Blair come on down, the price is right!

Blair turned up in his old stamping ground of Sedgefield on Tuesday to do to Gordon Brown exactly what he did to Iraq. It was a bit like Josef Mengele giving you a character reference. One thing's for certain though—Blair didn't give up lying for Lent.

Elves and

It was one step forward, two steps back for human rights as gay men won the right to donate blood and travellers at Dale Farm in Essex got a temporary reprieve from eviction but the US executed yet another innocent man and the DUP's Edwin Poots declared war on homosexuality, evolution ... and elves?

COURT HALTS DALE FARM EVICTIONS

Travellers win stay of execution as late injunction keeps their hopes alive – till Friday

UNITED STATES

Worldwide vigil for executed inmate

Troy Davis, 42, put to death after long battle to acquit him of murder

as right to kill up 1
"really honestly" believe

decided to rule out
r's smugness and me
ausing a conflagrat:
ng act of self-immo

nting the possibili
and confess all, re
devote the rest of

he Hague, he took a
d Lansdowne Partner

absolutely everyo

ssianic tendencies

g at his blatant h

evolution

Human rights have been given short shrift by the powers that be in recent days. The continuing attempts to forcibly expel travellers from their Essex homes could lead to the incongruous situation whereby Celebrity Big Brother winner Paddy Doherty is the only member of the travelling community not to be evicted.

Draconian sentences have been slapped on petty offenders for looting during the riots while Tory peers and Labour MPs stroll from prison after serving only a fraction of their jail terms for defrauding the public purse of thousands.

In the US, death row prisoner Troy Davis was executed this week despite massive amounts of evidence suggesting he was entirely innocent.

But on at least one issue there has been belated progress. A blanket ban on gay men giving blood has finally been scrapped by the Westminster government and the US has belatedly ditched its "don't ask, don't tell policy" on military enlistment.

But at a time when, in some parts of the globe, sanity is finally chipping away at prejudice and knee-jerk bigotry, at least on this one issue we can always rely on the bold men and women of the Democratic Unionist Party (DUP) to drag us back into the quagmire.

Yes, DUP Health Minister Edwin Poots bucked the trend by stating that the ban on gay blood donation should remain in

Northern Ireland because well, just because really.

It takes a special kind of evangelical arrogance for a farmer from Lisburn to dismiss out of hand the opinions and evidence provided by eminent scientists in the field and say he knows better.

But then this is the DUP, whose erstwhile leader Ian Paisley is in part remembered for his 1976 "save Ulster from sodomy" campaign to retain criminalisation of homosexuality.

He also memorably proclaimed in 2001 that line dancing was sinful and "caters to the lust of the flesh," with its "sexual gestures" and "touching."

The DUP track record on the issue of homosexuality is quite spectacular. In 2005 DUP Councillor Maurice Mills claimed that Hurricane Katrina was sent by God as "an act of judgement upon those who practise sodomy."

In February 2008, a certain Edwin Poots—yes, that one—condemned gay rugby team the Ulster Titans, claiming that the fact it was entirely made up of gay people was a form of "apartheid."

Which is a bit rich from a representative of a party which tried to prevent Catholics having civil rights and which saw nothing wrong with an entirely unionist Stormont.

Poots also attempted to impose a ban on civil partnerships taking place at Lisburn Civic Centre and opposed the granting of public funding for Gay Pride.

Also in 2008, DUP MLA Iris Robinson stated to a parliamentary committee that homosexuality was "viler" than child sex abuse.

You will no doubt recall that she was then exposed for having an illicit affair with a teenager over 30 years younger than herself.

Here's to you Mrs Robinson...

But to return to the redoubtable Mr Poots, let us examine his qualifications to be Health Minister. His website describes him as a "young earth creationist"—which means he believes the world was created in six days, that the bible is the literal word of God and that the earth is only 6,000 years old.

So we have the intriguing situation where someone in a position in which he wields substantial power over the medical profession doesn't believe in science and thinks that women were created from Adam's spare rib. And don't get him started on dinosaurs.

The site also proudly states that Poots is an "opponent of evolution." That's quite a bold statement, "opponent" of evolution, and leads to an intriguing metaphysical quandary—can you oppose something you don't believe exists?

That's like declaring you are an enemy of elves, except of course that unlike elves, evolution is real. He does however look like he's steadfastly refused to evolve so at least he's sticking to his principles.

Is the Pope

God's rottweiler
Pope Benedict went
all Che Guevara on
us with a stinging
broadside against
the evils of greed
and unemployment--
but somehow
forgot to
mention
his own
church's
role in
spreading
misery and
injustice

Pope tells world to end hunger

as right to kill up 1
"really honestly" believe

decided to rule out
r's smugness and mer
ausing a conflagrat:
ng act of self-immo

nting the possibili
and confess all, re
devote the rest of

"adviser" to JP Mo:

x a
tner

absolutely everyor

ssianic tendencies

g at his blatant h
d by the breathtak

tember 11 to the 1

ight years ago.

this egregious c

lay
cha
r s
ctn

fel
hin
be

is
ici

eek
th
pop
ks

bab
lf.

was

hose
not
on

thi

icul

...**communist?**

I s the Catholic church hypocritical? Does the Pope wear a funny hat? It appears that wonders will never cease. I knew that the Catholic church was into transubstantiation, but Il Papa himself seems to have morphed from a reactionary Islam-baiter into an eco-warrior and Che Guevara hybrid if his last edict is anything to go by.

Yes, God's rottweiler, the former Cardinal Ratzinger, now Pope Benedict, has unleashed a papal broadside against the sins of greed and the "amoral fascination with technological progress" in a 144-page encyclical. The latter is no real surprise—for the upper echelons of the church anything as technological as a telescope is an article of heresy and witchcraft. Just ask Galileo or Copernicus.

The encyclical starts off OK, with the pontiff explaining that the current economic crisis is clear proof of the pernicious effects of sin.

The fact that rapacious and avaricious capitalists are plundering ill-gotten gains from the poorest in society is not exactly a new concept, but then this is coming from a bloke who still believes the world was created in seven days. It's like grappling with quantum mechanics or string theory for him.

You'd be hard-pressed to argue that avarice and greed are wrong, but then you have to consider that the Catholic church plc is one of the wealthiest organisations on the planet and has primarily built that wealth by screwing it out of the poor and then making them feel guilty for not giving more. The words pot, kettle and black spring to mind.

But, as if that searing intellectual insight wasn't enough, now we get to the really fun bits.

Pope Benedict takes the opportunity, not entirely surprisingly, to proclaim that the only way out of this moral miasma is to adhere to Christian truth.

Whoa there, Benny—for a bloke who believes undoubtingly in a mythical entity for which there is absolutely no evidence and who told people in Africa and south America that condoms give you Aids to start bandying around words such as "truth" is a bit of a gamble, isn't it? It's called "faith" for a reason.

He then states that the iniquitous system of economics had led to "economic, social and political systems that trample upon personal and social freedom, and are therefore unable to deliver the justice that they promise."

Excuse me? This is the former head of the inquisition—a man who spent a large portion of his career persecuting and excommunicating liberation theologists and who rejected Vatican II, the radical attempt to drag the church kicking and screaming into the real world.

I would argue that the Catholic church hierarchy has done even less to help the poor and needy than Ronald McDonald. Nevertheless, the Pope then goes for the full house.

"Steady employment must be a goal for the countries," he writes, before expressing concerns that job insecurity makes it difficult to "forge coherent life plans." Not something he has to worry about, really.

In fact, what do you have to do to get kicked out of the Catholic church? Paedophile priests are still skulking from parish to parish, country to country like, well, like criminals.

Obviously all condemnation of capitalism is welcome and the Pope does have a lot of sway in certain parts of the world, but for him to be preaching on these issues is a bit like Silvio Berlusconi lecturing us on abstinence.

hearing I had reluctantly decided to rule
e sheer enormity of Blair's smugness and me
orm of chain reaction causing a conflagrati
nd therefore an unwitting act of self-immo

did was try to link September 11 to the Ir
cular claim didn't hold water eight years a
evidence to support this egregious claim be

hings were carried out mainly by

urprise, surprise. Tony Blair thinks he wa
illion people in an illegal war because he
e was right.

ell, that was worth £250k of public money
nows how much in inquiry salaries, wasn't

arles Manson probably really honestly bel:
every egomania   derer in

Lib Dems &
Other Liars

y'll probably be entitled 'How to shaft ab
e yourself."

Blair was always going to allow his messi
k—yet again.

as right to kill up
"really honestly" believes

Coalition of

decided to rule out
r's smugness and mer
conflagrat:

Quite a few people
voted Lib Dem
in the sincere
belief Nick
Clegg had
principles
and was maybe
even a bit
left-wing.
They soon
got a nasty
shock as he
hopped into bed
with David Cameron
quicker than
you can
say 'Tory
stooge'

POSH CHAPS TAKE POWER

Toffs Cameron and Clegg join forces for war on the workers

to JP Mo:
anded b

an inqu
he Hague, he took a
d Lansdowne Partner

Liberals cave in to war machine

Scent of power drives Clegg to embrace Trident and Afghan war

g at his blatant h
d by the breathtak

COALITION GOVERNMENT
Lib Dems drop key progressive policies

tember 11 to the

ght years ago.

+his egregious c

n probably really ho tly believed he was right to they
l ma
trigger some form of chain reaction ca agratio
and therefore an unwitting act of self-immola

the shilling

Well, that didn't take them long did it? By my reckoning about five seconds after the deal with the Tories was struck the Lib Dems hit the ejector button and jettisoned every alleged principle they professed to have.

Trident replacement? Okey-dokey! Immigration? You didn't think we were serious about that did you? Afghanistan? Where do we sign up?

They say power corrupts and absolute power corrupts absolutely but apparently the thrill of getting the scraps from the big table has roughly the same effect.

The interminable election was bad enough but the horse trading and now the nauseating mutual appreciation society that has vomited forth the Con-Dem coalition is truly repugnant.

I have always been of the view that you can tell when a politician is lying because their lips are moving but at least they usually try make some attempt to conceal the fact.

Every Lib Dem member of the coalition of the shill-ing has so far regurgitated the same platitudes with the rictus grin of someone who knows the bloke behind him has got a knife but doesn't know when it's going to be plunged into their back.

It's like they'd been told they'd won an all-expenses-paid trip to Disneyland but they had to take Josef Fritzl with them.

As for the Tories, I didn't think it was possible for David Cameron to get any more supercilious and odious. But his current incarnation as a cross between a comedy club compere and Paul Daniels is truly horrendous. "Ladies and gents, the next act is Vince Cable. You'll like him, but not a lot."

They've even wheeled out the blue-tinged behemoth Ken Clarke again. Surely he's past his sell-by date by now. Under the last Tory administration he managed to wreck health, education, the economy and millions of people's lungs with his role on the board of British American Tobacco.

As if that wasn't bad enough, now they've given him two jobs—Justice Secretary and Lord Chancellor.

This was a guy who was a member of the self-styled Tory "Cambridge mafia." Putting him in charge of justice is like giving Silvio Berlusconi the keys to a nunnery.

They even managed to resurrect Iain Duncan Smith as Secretary for Work and Pensions. I thought I'd imagined him.

The shots from inside the first Cabinet meeting looked like out-takes from The Island of Dr Moreau, the bits that were cut because they would terrify children and pensioners. And they should be terrified if the Tories get their way, which they undoubtedly will.

Anyone who believes that the Lib Dems are going to have any say in what goes on in this country should also be aware that the Oxford English Dictionary has no definition for gullible and that pyramid funds are a proven way to quadruple your income.

Nick Clegg wasn't a king-maker. He was a footstool so that Cameron could reach the top shelf during the midnight raid on the tuck shop.

To be honest, though, no-one should be too surprised at the Lib Dem volte-face. Most of them never believed in their policies in the first place, and they are probably still mildly surprised that anyone else did.

But this is the thing. Due to the moral bankruptcy of new Labour, the Lib Dems managed to portray themselves as the sole guardians of human rights and decency and people did believe they wanted to scrap Trident and pull out of Afghanistan.

Their shameless back-flip will come back to bite them the next time a by-election heaves into view or they need to deploy party activists to knock doors and sell their wares.

As the old adage goes—lie down with dogs, get put on the sex offenders register for life.

as right to kill up 1
"really honestly" believe

A sorry old

Poor Nick Clegg couldn't even get an apology right. First he had to say sorry for something he didn't even get round to doing-- calling opponents of gay marriage 'bigots'--then he earned himself national ridicule for a failed attempt to say sorry for breaking an election pledge not to raise tuition fees

decided to rule oul

POLITICS

Spineless Clegg 'sorry' for 2010 tuition pledge

Deputy Prime Minister apologises for making fees promise, not for breaking it in power

handed b

at an inqu
, he took a
wne Partner

absolutely everyor

Clegg backtracks on 'bigot' comment

tant h
eathtak

tember 11 to the 1

ight years ago.

this egregious c

spectacle

There are some questions to which humankind may never know the answer. Why are we here? What the hell is a duck-billed platypus? How has Nick Clegg still got a job?

Last week it appeared the craven Clegg had reached a personal nadir in his already kiboshed career with his spineless capitulation over the use of the B-word to criticise opponents of gay marriage.

It was not as much his "I'm Spartacus" moment as "I think you'll find that's him over there." Or to use a slightly more up-to-date example, standing there with an axe in his hand and saying: "I cannot tell a lie, it was a researcher who cut down the cherry tree."

But to assume he couldn't sink lower would be to underestimate the man—surely the only time those words have been written with regard to Clegg.

You'd have thought he might have learned a lesson about the perils of stabbing students in the back what with all those effigies of him being burned in the streets and all.

But no. Clegg recorded a video clip of him "apologising" for his shameful U-turn on tuition fees in which he spectacularly failed to apologise at all.

Presumably it was a video clip as he's holed up in a bomb-proof bunker somewhere trying to stop Vince Cable force-feeding him cyanide pills.

The two-and-a-half-minute clip is apparently to be part of a party political broadcast scheduled to be aired on Monday—although why they think they'll still have a party on Monday is beyond me. In it, a tieless Clegg—do they really think that will make them look cool? Although it may have been due to the fact he is a suicide risk—bleated what may have been intended to appear to be a mea culpa but was the exact opposite.

Many voters he had met were "angry and disappointed" at the party's decision to renege on its opposition to tuition fees, he said, with a fair degree of understatement—Millbank being open-planned, anyone?

He went on to say: "To those people, I say this: we made a promise before the election that we would vote against any rise in fees under any circumstances."

(We'll say anything to get into power)

"But that was a mistake. It was a pledge made with the best of intentions—but we shouldn't have made a promise we weren't absolutely sure we could deliver."

(We had no idea we'd ACTUALLY get into power!)

"I shouldn't have committed to a policy that was so expensive when there was no money around. Not least when the most likely way we'd end up in government was in coalition with Labour or the Conservatives, who were both committed to put fees up."

(It's really all their fault...)

"When you've made a mistake you should apologise. But more importantly, most important of all, you've got to learn from your mistakes. And that's what we will do."

(If Cameron can fake sincerity, so can I)

"I will never again make a pledge unless as a party we are absolutely clear about how we can keep it. I accept that won't be enough for everyone."

(I'm getting sacked at the party conference this week).

This column has a theory regarding the Lib Dem leader or, if you happen to be reading this on Sunday, probably ex-Lib Dem leader.

Namely, that so low has he sunk in the public opinion that he has recognised the futility of attempting to do anything right any more and has settled on becoming the WORST politician of all time.

He's given up on redeeming himself as he has now sunk so low that it would take an act of divine intervention to elevate him in the public mind. And after (almost) calling the archbishop a bigot that ain't going to happen any time soon.

December 31
2010
-----

is right to kill up 1
"really honestly" believe

Sinners and

2010 was the year
of volcanic ash,
BP oil and
the worst
British
government
in living
memory. So
competition was
stiff
when it
came to
handing
out
the gongs
for lies,
bigotry and
naked corruption--
literally, in one
winner's case

decided to rule out
r's smugness and me
ausing a conflagrat
g act of self-immo

"adviser" to JP Mo
after he handed b

ssianic tendencies

g at his blatant h
d by the breathtak

ight years ago.

this egregious c

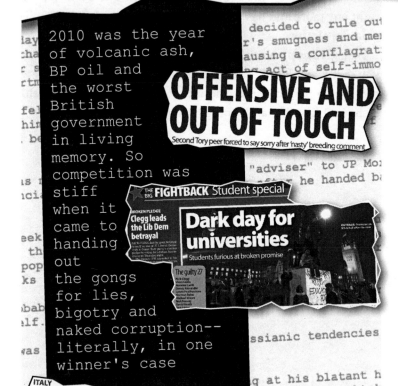

OFFENSIVE AND OUT OF TOUCH
Second Tory peer forced to say sorry after 'nasty' breeding comment

THE BIG **FIGHTBACK** Student special

BROKEN PLEDGE
Clegg leads the Lib Dem betrayal

Dark day for universities
Students furious at broken promise

The guilty 27

ITALY
Ex-Berlusconi ally calls for resignation
by Our Foreign Desk

THE estranged former ally of sleaze-tainted Italian Premier Silvio Berlusconi urged him to resign on Sunday for the good of the country and begin discussing a new government with a revised legislative agenda.

The premier, a media baron who controls or influences six of Italy's seven main TV channels, has been linked to Moroccan dancer Karima el Mahrug, who was just 17 when invited to a party at his house, and prostitute Nadia Macri, who said she was paid €10,000 (£8,600) have sex with him

new phase, with a new agenda and new programme, discussi note of other

probably really ho... ...lieved he was right to ...n't ... they ... ma...

:rigger some form of chain reaction cau... ...gratio
...and therefore an unwitting act of self-immola

sleazebags

It's been a funny old year with not many highs but plenty of lows—there was no cure for cancer but we did end up with a carcinogenic coalition.

We had no shortage of disasters with Icelandic ash clouds, the Gulf of Mexico oil spill and George Osborne's appointment as Chancellor.

Positives were few and far between, although the growing militancy of students, the annihilation of the BNP in Barking and Dagenham and Blairite lackey David Miliband not being elected Labour leader were all causes for celebration.

So as we bid goodbye to 2010 it is time to pay proper dues to those who have stood out in their given fields and gone above and beyond the call of duty over the last 12 months.

Without further ado, this column presents its new—and possibly only—Annual Awards of the Year:

First up is the **Berlusconi Award for Commitment to Political Ideology**. There was only ever one real candidate for this particular gong. Yes, that's right—Nick Clegg, come on down. Clegg and his cronies jettisoned any shred of liberal veneer they had clung to in opposition to form the Coalition of the Shilling. Who would have thought a millionaire former public schoolboy would turn out to be a Tory?

The **King Herod Award for Child Development**. This award is split three ways this year because none of the major political parties have clean hands when it comes to the travesty of tuition fees. Labour introduced them, the Tories trebled them and the Lib Dems back-flipped like a clockwork monkey.

The **Norman Tebbit Award for Community Cohesion** goes to ... those perennial favourites the West Midlands Police who—not content with beating up and fitting up black and Asian people in the Midlands—decided to go all Man from UNCLE by fitting spy cameras across an entire community before being forced into a grovelling apology.

The other leading contenders, the Metropolitan Police, were disqualified from competition this year as they now appear to be totally indiscriminate when it comes to meting out violence on the streets of the capital.

The **Orange Order Traditional Route Award** goes to the Tories for ditching their frankly risible attempt to appear to be the new caring sharing party and reverting to type so totally that if you close your eyes you could swear it was 1984.

The **Rio Ferdinand Award for Ill-advised Public Speaking**. There was hot competition for this particular prize this year. Tory peer Lord Young made a strong bid with not one but two entries, as did Ukip Euro-warrior Godfrey Bloom with his sterling work in the field of Anglo-Germanic relations.

But in the end they were both edged out by another true-blue knee-jerk bigot, newly selected peer Howard Flight, the former banker and Tory party chair who brayed that welfare cuts would encourage the poor to breed.

The **Richard Nixon International Memorial Award for Propriety in Public Office**. Again quite a tricky one to whittle down, what with MPs claiming for duck islands and moat cleaning, Nicolas Sarkozy being embroiled in the L'Oréal scandal and the Ivory Coast's Laurent Gbagbo refusing to leave office after being trounced in the elections and arresting every opposition politician he can get his hands on.

But when it comes to scandal there can be only one choice. Yes, that's right, the Sultan of Sleaze himself, Silvio Berlusconi. Prostitutes, Bunga Bunga, underage consorts, vote-rigging and telling earthquake victims to enjoy their camping holiday. All in a day's work for Italy's Teflon tyrant.

And last but by no means least we come to the **Changing Rooms Award for Urban Redesign**—a new award this year, and its inaugural winners have to be the plucky tuition fees protesters for their spectacular remodelling job on Tory headquarters.

Government doesn't get much more open than that. Happy new year!

hearing I had reluctantly decided to rule

e sheer enormity of Blair's smugness and me

form of chain reaction causing a conflagrati

nd therefore an unwitting act of self-immo

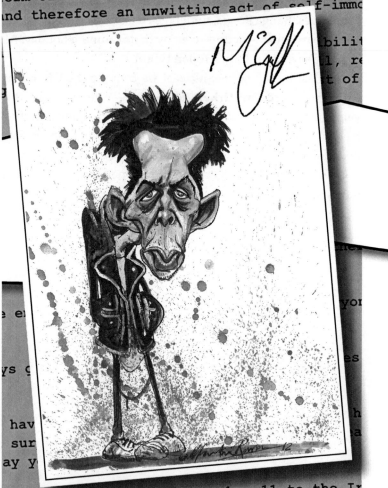

did was try to link September 11 to the Ir

cular claim didn't hold water eight years a

evidence to support this egregious claim be

were carried out mainly by

urprise, surprise. Tony Blair thinks he wa
illion people in an illegal war because he
e was right.

ell, that was worth £250k of public money
nows how much in inquiry salaries, wasn't

arles Manson probably really honestly beli
every egomania   derer in

Warmongers

How (ex-future) President Blair stops traffic...

Blair was always going to allow his messi
—yet again.

Cameron gets

Every PM wants the chance to act Churchillian for the cameras and the bombing of-- sorry, 'intervention in'-- Libya offered the Tory toff an opportunity to talk tough on tyranny while slaughtering innocent civilians and shaking the hands of some very dodgy dictators

MILITARY MISTAKES: Prime Minister David Cameron wants to pursue war in Libya - despite ongoing protests against

COMMONS VOTE

'Shameless' MPs rubber-stamp Libya air assault

Stop the War criticises 'gung-ho' support for war

Well, David Cameron has finally got his Thatcher moment with his imperialist "intervention" in Libya. The glee with which he and his French counterpart Nicolas Sarkozy spout their posturing pronouncements of moral righteousness is all too evident.

If this goes on long enough he'll probably turn up on a British army base in a tank wearing a headscarf.

There was never any doubt he would begin the bombing of Libya the first chance he got. He's been itching for a war and he didn't really care where.

Scotland is probably breathing a sigh of relief—they've got oil and according to the Tories are in league with Muammar Gadaffi after releasing Abdelbaset al-Megrahi on compassionate grounds.

It's been ages since the Tories had a war they could definitively claim was theirs without Tony Blair hogging the war crimes spotlight.

Afghanistan and Iraq are no fun. The Tories were just enthusiastic cheerleaders for those and irritatingly, in the case of Afghanistan, it won't go away.

Every world leader desperately wants to be a Churchillian-style wartime prime minister or president.

Thatcher invaded a small island that barely anyone in Britain had ever heard of in a blatant—and successful—bid for re-election.

From the hysteria of the fourth estate at the time, you could have been forgiven for thinking the Malvinas were off the coast of Shetland not Argentina.

Blair invaded so many countries it's difficult to keep count—Iraq twice, Kosovo, Sierra Leone, Afghanistan ... but then he had God on his side.

Bill Clinton, who many deluded people still insist was a good guy just because his presidency was sandwiched between those of two reactionary fundamentalist Christian cretins, even bombed a Sudanese aspirin factory merely to distract unwanted press attention from a fellatio-related scandal.

And don't get me started on the Bush double act—they had wars, respectively, on drugs and emotions.

As allied forces continue to rain bloody death on civilians, Cameron is strutting around like a pugnacious bantam cock.

His specious claims of moral superiority can be blown out of the water with one simple point.

If his aim, as regurgitated ad nauseam, was really to stand up for democracy against tyranny, why haven't they launched all-out assaults on Bahrain, Yemen, Qatar and particularly Saudi Arabia?

The house of Saud has actually sent armed troops into another sovereign state, Bahrain, albeit at the behest of its own dictatorial regime.

Hundreds of demonstrators have been—and continue to be—gunned down and blown to smithereens by the Bahraini regime to nothing more than a "tut tut" from the bold defenders of democracy.

But then they were using weapons flogged to them on very generous payment terms by Britain and other UN nations, so they probably saw it more as field testing.

And anyway, the cheques probably haven't cleared yet.

The US is sticking to its well-established game plan in Libya. They've already started strafing civilians who were actively trying to help them.

One can't help recalling the stage-managed fiasco of the "rescue" of Private Jessica Lynch, where doctors who had saved her life and were trying to return her to her own forces at great personal risk were attacked by US troops.

Gadaffi is an old-fashioned pantomime villain—"The people are behind me!" "Oh no they're not."

In recent weeks he has said: "I am like the Queen of England" and "We put our fingers in the eyes of those who doubt that Libya is ruled by anyone other than its people."

He is a brutal dictator engaged in the violent suppression of his own people, but the US and Britain have no claim to moral superiority.

They have slaughtered hundreds of thousands of innocent civilians in Iraq and Afghanistan, and used indiscriminate torture to further their goals.

And while we're on the subject of hundreds of thousands of people taking to the streets to overthrow egotistical leaders who persecute the poor and who ignore the wishes of their own people, Cameron doesn't need to look much further than his own doorstep.

as right to kill up t

"really honestly" believe

War crimes

decided to rule out

r's smugness and mei

ausing a conflagrat:

ng act of self-immo

lay
cha
r s
rtm

fel
hir
be

Perhaps at divine
behest Blair
announced he
would give
the £4.6m
advance for
his memoirs
to a centre
for injured
soldiers.
A generous
offer from anyone
else--but not when
you're earning £20m
a year and you're
the reason
there are
so many
maimed
soldiers around

IRAQ WAR

Blair pledge does not make up for war, say activists

TONY Blair's attempt to salve his conscience will be little comfort to injured troops, peace campaigners stated yesterday after he pledged to create the profits from his memoirs to a new sports centre for wounded soldiers.

CHARITY BID: Blair has offered £4.5 million for a sports centre for injured soldiers

he stand at an inqu
he Hague, he took a
d Lansdowne Partner

Blair 'should be in jail, not making money'

cies

is r
ici

eek
th
pop
ks

bab
lf.

vas

g at his blatant h
d by the breathtak

hose
not
on

thi

tember 11 to the]

ight years ago.

icul

this egregious c

evangelist

So the arch war criminal Tony Blair has said he will donate the advance for his no doubt wildly self-aggrandising and revisionist memoirs to a sports centre for injured troops.

Well, when you're on an estimated £20 million a year you don't tend to worry about the small change, do you?

Maybe he's been having one of his late-night talks with Him upstairs again and it was pointed out to him that he'd be saying Hail Marys for the rest of his life otherwise.

Blair seems to have the unwavering belief that he can manipulate public opinion and rewrite history at his whim, a trait so common in his fellow evangelists such as Jerry Falwell and Pat Robertson. Falwell, Robertson and their odious ilk usually only warp and manipulate the bible to suit their own ends and dupe their credulous faithful.

This is a text that, whether you believe in it or not, is wildly ambiguous and couched in archaic language which many feel free to interpret however they wish. A book dealing with the mythical adventures of a cast of characters who, if they ever existed, are unlikely to have you up for misrepresentation. It would be like being sued by Asterix and Obelix.

And of course evangelists always use the get-out clause that no-one can prove that their interpretation—which in a roundabout way uncannily always leads to calls for greater donations—is wrong because it's a question of faith.

As the late, great comic Bill Hicks noted, these are people who state categorically that the bible is the word of God then say: "I think what the Lord meant to say was..."

Like Blair, Robertson and Falwell used their professed "faith" to claim some deeply repulsive things.

Most recently in Robertson's case he claimed that the Haitian earthquake was due to the country having signed a "pact with the devil." In Falwell's case to demonise gays, Muslims and, er ... the Teletubbies.

Well, they say the Lord moves in mysterious ways ... and no more so than when "interpreted" through the mouth of a racist, homophobic con man like Falwell.

But compared with these two Blair is attempting to pull off a sleight-of-hand trick that David Blaine would be proud of.

He's trying to rewrite a history that we all witnessed for ourselves. We know he's lied repeatedly. We know he led Britain into an illegal war in order to cosy up to the US.

This latest in a long list of attempts to define himself in the public eye as a "pretty straight kind of guy" reeks of the cynicism which clings to him like cheap aftershave making people gag wherever he goes.

But then he has had a great deal of encouragement to believe that he can wipe the slate clean. His farcical appointment as Middle East peace envoy being the most obvious example, closely followed by the seemingly never-ending corporate gigs and lecture tours around the US and elsewhere.

The money, despite the dubious motivation for the donation, may well do some good but that doesn't let him off the hook. In one very obvious way he has not changed in the slightest. He still doesn't give a damn about the hundreds of thousands of Iraqi and Afghan civilians slaughtered as a result of his jingoistic adventurism.

Where's the donation to ease their suffering?

Blair himself, in common with Bush, has said he will answer to a higher authority. If there's any justice they will—and it will be at The Hague.

Half-baked

Warmongering ex-PM Tony Blair got the softest of rides when he appeared at the Iraq inquiry to declare he was right about everything all along-- even Saddam Hussein's phantom WMD-- after sneaking in through a side door to avoid being shamed by crowds of anti-war protesters

Blair faces war panel

Former PM refuses to admit he was wrong over Saddam WMD

Storm of protest as unrepentant Blair slinks into Iraq inquiry through a side door to avoid the public, citing security fears

POOR EXCUSE

grilling

urprise, surprise. Tony Blair thinks he was right to kill up to a million people in an illegal war because he "really honestly" believed he was right.

Well, that was worth £250k of public money in police protection plus God knows how much in inquiry salaries, wasn't it?

Charles Manson probably really honestly believed he was right too, as has every egomaniacal mass murderer in history. It doesn't mean they are. Or that they should be allowed to do it.

Prior to yesterday's hearing I had reluctantly decided to rule out the possibility that the sheer enormity of Blair's smugness and mendacity would trigger some form of chain reaction causing a conflagration in the Y-front department and therefore an unwitting act of self-immolation.

Likewise, I felt fairly confident in discounting the possibility that he would throw himself at the inquiry's mercy and confess all, rending his garments and beating his chest pledging to devote the rest of his life to doing good.

That much was made clear when he became an "adviser" to JP Morgan and Zurich Financial Services about two seconds after he handed back the keys of No 10.

Then this week, mere days before he took the stand at an inquiry which most people think should be conducted in The Hague, he took a huge £200,000-a-pop wedge from London hedge fund Lansdowne Partners to give private talks to its employees.

They'll probably be entitled "How to shaft absolutely everyone and still love yourself."

No, Blair was always going to allow his messianic tendencies to run amok—yet again.

But even those who have spent years railing at his blatant hypocrisy must have been not surprised but still staggered by the breathtaking mendacity on display yesterday.

The first thing he did was try to link September 11 to the Iraqi regime. Again. That particular claim didn't hold water eight years ago. There is absolutely no evidence to support this egregious claim because it is patently untrue.

The World Trade Centre bombings were carried out mainly by religious fundamentalist Saudi nationals, funded by Osama bin Laden.

Iraq and Saudi Arabia hated each other, mainly because Iraq was—and I emphasise was—the only secular state in the Middle East.

Of course the country is riddled with al-Qaida and God knows who else now, but only because of the war. You can't claim a country is a terrorist threat on the basis that you're damn sure it will be by the time you're finished with it.

That's like saying there are weapons of mass destruction in a country because by the time you've tampered with all the intelligence it will look like there are—oh...

You only have to look at the way the attempted justifications have gone—WMD, 45 minutes, regime change and Saddam was a bad man.

Then the government shifted towards saying the media had overegged the 45-minute claim, to if Saddam had had WMD it would have been very bad, to the spectacular claim made by Blair yesterday that the belief that Saddam had WMD was not a "counterintuitive notion."

OK, so we went to war on a notion now did we? How does that work? "My elbow's playing up—must be time to bomb Iraq!"

But the most glaring indication of Blair's culpability was his decision to skulk into the inquiry through a back door at the crack of dawn rather than face the people he had lied to, conned and patronised throughout his term in office.

Rather than face members of the Iraqi community whose country he tore apart, whose families he slaughtered because— as we learned today—he felt it was right.

Blair may one day be held to account for his crimes against humanity and we may have our day in court. But this most definitely wasn't it.

as right to kill up 1
"really honestly" believed

Move over,

From Iraq to Bloody Sunday, Blair's memoir turned out to be the most inventive work of fantasy fiction since Baron Munchausen was in his pomp. And let's not even mention the romantic bits

decided to rule out
r's smugness and me
ausing a conflagrat
ng act of self-imm

nting the possibili
and confess all, re
devote the rest of

"adviser" to JP Mor
s after he handed b

Unrepentant Blair releases memoirs

Former PM uses spotlight to call for Iran attack and promote 'small state'

ember 11 to the 1

ight years ago.

JK Rowling

This week has seen the publication of the most hotly anticipated work of fiction since the last Harry Potter book.

So what have we learned with the publication of the life and times of Anthony Charles Lynton Blair, except that he's a bigger liar and fantasist than ever?

We've seen some whitewashes recently—the Butler report, the Hutton report, the probing at the Iraq inquiry are three which immediately spring to mind—all of which have one thing in common: they saved Blair's blushes.

But there was no need to hire a retired Whitehall mandarin to bleach his smalls prior to public inspection this time.

No, when it comes to revisionism and self-aggrandising Blair has shown himself to be rivalled by no man with the possible exception of Baron Munchausen. A Journey, he grandiloquently entitled his tome, though it's not so much a mea culpa as a "what, me?"

What to make of this over-the-counter ordure? For reasons of taste we will gloss over the romantic elements of the book much in the way that Blair has glossed over any reference to wrongdoing or duplicity on his part. Although there is at least one reference to him "devouring" Cherie's love "like an animal" and an equally alarming Women in Love-style homoerotic reference to Blair and Gordon Brown being like "two lovers" who couldn't wait to get down to lovemaking, conjuring up the queasy image of the two of them wrestling naked on the rug in No 10.

But his bid for Barbara Cartland's pink-tinged tiara aside, his attempt to cast himself as a reluctant hero facing the forces of darkness shows just how self-deluded he really is.

One of the most bizarre excerpts shows that he deliberately sabotaged the fox-hunting ban because he did not know the depth of feeling it would evoke.

Blair claiming that public outrage swayed his opinion? Two million people on the streets didn't "sway" his opinion about the war, did it? But a few uppity horsey types complaining that they were being deprived of their "sport" and prevented from hounding an innocent animal to its death and he backflips quicker than a Romanian gymnast on steroids.

And speaking of the war, Blair claimed he was desperately sorry for those who died and indeed had wept tears for them, but surprise, surprise, won't apologise for it.

He even has the gall to tell people to "keep an open mind"—which one can't help feeling is advice he should probably have heeded himself in 2003. Then in time-honoured fashion he played the "I'm just an ordinary guy" card by admitting that he turned to drink to deal with the stresses of the job. Not "excessively excessively," he is quick to state.

Although it appears that Blair may have been indulging in a cheeky Vimto or two while penning his book. Having done his best to play down the achievements of Northern Ireland secretary Mo Mowlam in bringing about the peace process and claim the glory for himself, he makes a further bid to boast of his earnest intervention, this time with the Saville inquiry into Bloody Sunday—but he drops the ball spectacularly.

He states: "To assuage nationalist opinion and under pressure from the Irish, I also ordered an inquiry into the Bloody

Sunday shootings in 1972, when British troops had opened fire on protesters in Belfast, killing a number of people."

Belfast! Not Derry then? If you're trying to claim credit for something you would think you might actually try to get your facts straight.

Further proof if any were needed that whether it be the murdered people of Derry or the hundreds of thousands of Iraqi and Afghan civilians slaughtered in his name, Blair couldn't care less.

Sympathy for

On the 30th anniversary of the Falklands war ending, and amid continuing wrangles over the islands' future, former Downing St press officer Ian Kydd set himself Mission Impossible--trying to convince us Thatcher was sick with worry at the thought of her Argentinian victims

ISLANDS DISPUTE RUMBLES ON

Argentina pushes Falklands claim

President makes her case to the UN decolonisation committee

as right to kill up
"really honestly" believe

decided to rule out
r's smugness and mer
ausing a conflagrat:
ng act of self-immo

nting the possibili
and confess all, re
devote the rest of

"adviser" to JP Mor

absolutely everyor

ssianic tendencies

g at his blatant h
d by the breathtak

tember 11 to the

ght years ago.

this egregious c

the devil?

trigger some form of chain reaction ca... ...agratio ...ant and therefore an unwitting act of self-immola

This week saw the online publication of criminal records archives dating back to the Victorian era. The Dorset prison admission and discharge registers 1782-1901 and Dorset calendar of prisoners 1854-1904 detailed names and ages of those convicted and the nature of offences committed. They also contain mug shots of convicts.

Among the "felons" recorded are 18-year-old George Pill who was sentenced to six weeks' hard labour for the heinous crime of stealing a donkey. Something that would get you a badge of honour in the Bullingdon Club.

Another shows that a Charles Wood was sentenced to a month in prison for "refusing to quit the beer-house." Again…

Samuel Baker, aged 73, was sentenced to nine months' hard labour after being convicted of breaking into a house and stealing some vests, a pair of stockings and two brushes.

Nicolas Robinson, 23, of Borough, south-east London, was sentenced to three months' imprisonment for stealing a bottle of water.

The publication will no doubt prove a source of gallows humour (literally in some cases) and titillation for some, and will probably be seen with dewy-eyed nostalgia as a reminder of the halcyon days of British justice for readers of the Daily Heil.

Many more, Tories and liberals both, will point to such draconian sentencing and, for different reasons, argue that it illustrates how much better and more lenient today's justice system is.

They'd be wrong. You see, while the majority of the afore-mentioned "crimes" occurred in the 19th century, the last was committed less than 12 months ago.

The fact that it doesn't look out of place alongside the historical convictions tells us all we need to know about our so-called civilised society.

Thousands of people have been convicted and sentenced to lengthy terms of imprisonment as a result of their somewhat liberal interpretation of the phrase "everything must go" during the riots last August.

Also last year, dozens of people were arrested for the apparently treasonable offence of not liking the royal family in advance of the nauseating nuptials.

Conversely Tony Blair and Margaret Thatcher continue to remain at liberty. This week marked the 30th anniversary of the Malvinas war and therefore the sinking of the Belgrano for which Thatcher was lucky to avoid a trip to the Hague.

And to mark the occasion we had the latest toadying attempt to airbrush the old fascist's reputation.

Readers may recall a recent risible attempt to suggest that the arch-Tory bigot was a human being as opposed to Davros with a handbag after documents emerged claiming she was anguished over the 1981 Irish hunger strikes.

This week we had the next instalment in what this column likes to think of as Mission Improbable.

Former Tory press officer—for which read spin doctor—Ian Kydd made the claim that shortly before midnight on June 14 1982, a few hours after a ceasefire had been announced, the warmongering Thatcher had privately told him that her thoughts were with the mothers of the Argentinian conscripts.

Kydd states that Thatcher told him: "I am relieved I will be able to go to sleep tonight without worrying about those terrible Exocets—and I'm sure Argentine mothers will feel the same."

Well, perhaps you shouldn't have started a spurious war to get yourself re-elected then.

And while we're on the subject, her son was probably getting lost in the desert or flogging arms to some tinpot dictator at the time so it's not really the same thing.

As claims go Kydd's is up there with ex-royal butler, bulimic-botherer and rampant self-publicist Paul Burrell saying that the Queen had warned him of "dark forces at work."

Or Cameron claiming that he didn't strike a deal with Murdoch to get him into power.

s right to kill up 1
"really honestly" believ

Sincerely,

As BAE Systems
kicked off its
annual attempt
to woo fresh-
faced students
to the dark side
the Star got hold
of a top-secret
memo regarding the
arms industry's
inexplicably poor
public reputation

lay
:ha
r s
rtm

fel
hir
. be

is
ici

eek

decided to rule out
r's smugness and me
ausing a conflagrat:
ng act of self-immo

nting the possibili
and confess all, re
devote the rest of

"adviser" to JP Mo:
s after he handed ba

he stand at an inqu
he Hague, he took a
d Lansdowne Partner

ARMS TRADE

Students called on to shun BAE

UNETHICAL: BAE Systems targets students at university careers fairs

p
k

absolutely everyor

ssianic tendencies

g at his blatant h
d by the breathtak

hose
not
on

thi

tember 11 to the 1

ight years ago.

icul:

this egregious c

Murder PLC

Never let it be said that this column does not go the extra mile for a scoop! Yes, by exercising cunning, stealth and a fair amount of deception your scribe has managed to obtain the following top-secret document from an insider in the arms industry.

At great personal risk, both physical and financial—and which we're pretty sure we cannot claim back on expenses— your intrepid reporter met the shady individual in question in a central London sushi restaurant (what could possibly go wrong with a plan like that?).

In the best traditions of the espionage thriller, code words were exchanged, documents and incriminating photos changed hands, and strange, fizzing tea was imbibed. I only hope it was worth it...

Internal Memo Merchants of Death PLC —

Dear employee, we have been noticing of late that, as bizarre as this may sound, our noble profession is receiving what could only be described as negative public attention.

Our mission to empower and protect the human race through sales of weapons of mass destruction to the highest bidder has apparently been misunderstood by the pinko liberals and tree huggers.

Criticism has even been made of our long-standing policy of loitering around educational establishments offering gainful employment to pupils.

It is reaching the point where being an arms dealer is being viewed in the same light as pederasty.

Honestly! We don't molest children, we just kill them.

For the above reasons we have decided to introduce the following customer-based questionnaire system in order to allow us to more usefully target our client base.

Dear Sir/Madam/Your Royal Highness,

We notice you or someone in your family/government/dictatorship (delete as applicable) has purchased one or more of our products in recent months.

As part of our never-ending pursuit of customer satisfaction, we at the cutting edge of murderous technology at astronomical prices would appreciate it if you could take a moment to complete our consumer survey. Please take the time to answer the following questions, if you still possess appendages enough to do so.

Perhaps you have had the thrill of observing our product close up? In which case your input—although less interesting to us unless YouTube footage is available—will at least make up the numbers for this survey.

How did you first discover our product?

A) Sleazy bloke in dark glasses and suit sidled up to you during a ministerial visit.

B) Your Cayman Islands bank account became swollen by an additional six-figure sum.

C) You are a regular subscriber to Deathdealer magazine.

D) Heard a loud bang, looked up and saw your house had gone.

What impact has our product had on your life?

A) Increased feelings of security and virility.

B) Allowed you to invade next-door neighbour.

C) Quashed all internal dissent.
D) Slaughtered your whole family.

What improvements do you feel could be made to our product?
A) More back-handers.
B) Greater kill-per-buck ratio.
C) Relabelling as machine parts.
D) not giving them to bloodthirsty tyrants.

NB: any survey returned with mostly Ds will be instantly shredded and the respondee's details passed on to the security services/religious police.

This month those charming people at BAE Systems began their annual recruitment campaign at careers fairs in universities around the country aiming to turn naive young students to the dark side with promises of oodles of ready cash.

I know quite a lot of students are pretty apathetic but surely not to the extent that they get given a free pen and suddenly decide that what they want to do in life is end other people's.

How exactly do you pitch a job like that? Do you have negligible standards of decency and a moral compass permanently pointing south? Do you have a ruthless desire to accumulate money and don't care if it's liberally daubed in gore and bits of children? Perhaps you are a middle child harbouring a seething resentment towards humanity because you feel overlooked?

Then have we got a career for you! It's either that or join the Tory Party.

hearing I had reluctantly decided to rule
sheer enormity of Blair's smugness and me
form of chain reaction causing a conflagrati
and therefore an unwitting act of self-immo

bilit
l, re
t of

g

e

yo

ys g

es

hav

sur

ay y

did was try to link September 11 to the Ir
cular claim didn't hold water eight years a
evidence to support this egregious claim be

were carried out mainly by

urprise, surprise. Tony Blair thinks he wa
illion people in an illegal war because he
e was right.

ell, that was worth £250k of public money
nows how much in inquiry salaries, wasn't

arles Manson probably eally honestly bel:
every egomani derer in

Royals, Dictators
& Fascists

U-Turn latest...

y'll probably be entitled how to smart ab
e yourself."

Blair was always going to allow his messi
k—yet again.

s right to kill up
"really honestly" believe

Torturers'

decided to rule out
r's smugness and me
ausing a conflagrat
ng act of self-immo

nting the possibili
and confess all, re
devote the rest of

Our royal family
has decades of
form when it comes
to pressing the
flesh with dodgy
dictators--but even
so Prince Andrew
raised eyebrows
by cuddling up
to a string of
corrupt regimes
in his role as
a global trade
lobbyist

lay
cha
r s
rtm

fel
hir
be

is
ici

eek
th
pop
ks

bab
lf.

was

hose
not
on

thi

icul

POLITICS

Prince's ties to despots under fire

Activists call for sacking over trade
envoy's conduct on business trips

ssianic tendencies

g at his blatant h
d by the breathtak

tember 11 to the

ight years ago.

this egregious c

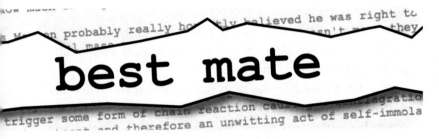

best mate

W ell! Who'd have thought it? A member of our esteemed and noble royal family embroiled in a scandal involving despots, merchants of death and sex offenders! Say it isn't true!

I for one am shocked. If you can't trust a member of the Windsor clan not to cosy up to dodgy dictators what can you do? All right, there was that unfortunate love-in between Edward VIII and Hitler...

And of course there is that minor issue regarding the lineage of Princess Michael of Kent—what with her dad being in the SS and everything...

Come to think of it, there was also that invitation to card-carrying psychopath and alleged cannibal Idi Amin to dine with the Queen...

Oh, and then I do seem to remember an embarrassing incident where Prince Charles was snapped shaking hands with Robert Mugabe ... although that was more of a Jeremy Beadle moment to be fair.

He's a one that Mugabe isn't he, eh? Always playing little pranks. Hilarious japes like starving his people and brutally repressing any form of democratic opposition.

But in Charles's defence it's a little-known fact that centuries of inbreeding can produce a neurological condition where the sufferer is unable to distinguish between members of their former colonies.

Not to be outdone the Duke of York, apparently keen to bolster his image as a boorish ignoramus, has decided to really push the boat out this time.

Yes, Airmiles Andy—as he is jocularly known—when not getting us to pay for a helicopter trip to the links has been doing his patriotic duty for Mum and country schmoozing autocrats and arms dealers the world over.

It's that kind of dedication to money—er, I mean duty—that makes the national bosom swell with pride. And so noble is the Duke that he does all this out of the goodness of his heart with only a whacking great expense account to ease the burden.

He's loyal to his friends as well. Some, less well-bred individuals might have distanced themselves from their old pal billionaire Jeffrey Epstein after he was done for soliciting underage sex and banged up. But not the bold Andy. He stayed straight and true and even offered the convicted sex offender a chance to redeem himself by loaning Fergie 15 grand!

But then compared to some of his other friends a bit of pederasty probably seems like light relief.

Showing that legendary impartiality for which the monarchy are famed Andy has also cuddled up to Gurbanguly Berdimuhamedow, president of Turkmenistan—described as one of the most corrupt countries in the world.

He has also racked up quite a few frequent flyer points on trips to Azerbaijan. Andy has been to the country three times in as many years in "a private capacity" and at least half a dozen times as a "trade envoy."

Neither of these regimes are strangers to a spot of recreational human rights abusing.

In relation to Turkmenistan Amnesty International states: "The whereabouts of dozens of victims of forced disappearances in 2002 remain unknown. Prisoners of conscience continue to be imprisoned for peacefully expressing their beliefs." Just the kind of bloke you want to do business with then!

He has said that he sees Azerbaijan as a country of "great opportunities." He's right: there are opportunities round every corner. The opportunity to be tortured, the opportunity to do what you're told or else, the opportunity to get your head stoved in for standing up for your rights... It's a veritable smorgasbord of brutality, corruption and repression.

The royal globetrotter is described in the country's national media as "the dear guest" which if anything is an understatement. He's costing us a bleeding fortune.

as right to kill up
"really honestly" believed

The nitwit

2012, the year of
the anniversary--
which meant fawning
praise for the
royal sponger-
in-chief and
a wildly
inappropriate
hijacking of a
great novelist

decided to rule ou
r's smugness and me
ausing a conflagrat
ng act of self-immo

the possibili

JUBILEE

Miliband puts out sickening Queen tribute

he stand at an inqu
he Hague, he took a
d Lansdowne Partner

absolutely everyo

ssianic tendencies

HAPPY BIRTHDAY: Dickens

LITERATURE

Dickens 'more relevant than ever' in Britain

g at his blatant h
d by the breathtak

tember 11 to the

ight years ago.

this egregious c

probably really h... ...ieved he was right to ...n't ... they ...

papers

rigger some form of chain reaction cau... ...gratio ...therefore an unwitting act of self-immola

Twenty-twelve is indeed the year of the anniversary—and by extension, the year of the fatuous quote. We have had the usual fawning tributes to the scrounger-in-chief on her 60th year of state-funded indolence.

That's a long time to be on state handouts and she gets child benefits in the form of the civil list. If only the Tories had some sort of back-to-work programme she could go on—perhaps a scheme with a moniker encapsulating the essence of employment and fairness. A few weeks stacking shelves in Tesco's for a pittance might do her and her good-for-nothing gaggle of grifters some good. "Charles Windsor to aisle 12, there's been a spillage in the sanitary products department."

But no. Just listen to this verbal diarrhoea from the so-called leader of the opposition in the Commons this week. "Her Majesty's life reminds us of the true value of service and her reign is indeed a golden thread that links people within and across the generations," Ed Miliband said.

Indeed it does link people—in subservience, poverty and gross inequality. But he didn't stop there. "In these moments we are reminded that we are far more than just disparate individuals and communities but a nation with a shared sense of purpose and integrity," he toadied. To what exactly is he in opposition?

It's instructive to note mere days after scientists stated that we are all descended from worms that some people seem to be nostalgic for a time when their backbones were but an aspiration.

But of course there are other much more important commemorations afoot this year and as ever there are those only too eager to capitalise on the fact.

This year marks 200 years since the birth of legendary author, journalist and social reform champion Charles Dickens. What better way to mark the event than for his words to be hijacked by a car insurance salesman?

Henry Engelhardt, boss of those well-known philanthropists Admiral Insurance, extended the list of Dickens's talents to include soothsayer and oracle.

"It was the best of times, it was the worst of times, it was the age of wisdom, it was the age of foolishness," he quoth. "How did Mr Dickens know, nearly 200 years ago, that his words could be used to describe Admiral's 2011 year?"

Now Dickens predicted many things and had an unusually enlightened view on social issues. I'm sure he would have had particularly erudite views on the modern shyster insurers who fleece us with premiums and then do their utmost to avoid paying out, getting rich on the misery and fear of others.

It's intriguing that he referenced A Tale of Two Cities with its prominent themes of revolution, social justice and attempted redemption through self-sacrifice which, let's face it, are not exactly synonymous in most people's minds with the insurance industry. Guillotining in a public square, however...

Having apparently decided that he had not besmirched the ideas and memory of Dickens enough, he then went on to quote from Oliver Twist.

Boasting of his firm's record profits last year he said: "If this is, as Dickens put it, the winter of despair, then I say: 'Please, sir, may I have some more?'"

It takes a particular brand of odious cynicism to take the words of a starving orphan and use them to call for even greater wads of cash for you and your cronies.

This year also marks the 300th anniversary of the birth of French philosopher and radical Jean-Jacques Rousseau. I can just see the adverts now. "Man is born free, but he is everywhere in chains. If you want us to make sure they stay that way call G4S now on 0800..."

February 19 2011

Prince joins

as right to kill up 1
"really honestly" believe

The Con-Dems may be hacking their way through the NHS, the welfare state and the public sector but Prince Charles knew the real issue on which to take a stand-- the endangered red squirrel

decided to rule out
r's smugness and mer
ausing a conflagrat:
ng act of self-immo

nting the possibili
fess all, re
rest of

FOREST PRIVATISATION

Woods sell-off bad news for rare wildlife

ed ba

an inqu
e Hague he took a
d Lansdowne Partner

absolutely everyor

ssianic tendencies

g at his blatant h
d by the breathtak

tember 11 to the]

ght years ago.

this egregious c

the reds

The country is in turmoil. The Tories are butchering the public sector with more glee than Sweeney Todd on two-for-one day. The bankers are lining their pockets with yet more of our money having rejigged their wage/bonus ratio to lucrative effect.

Millions are out of work and the coalition is slashing their benefits like a lunatic cutting adrift the lifeboats on the Titanic. It is fortunate then that in our time of dire need a saviour has stepped forward to take a stand on the key issue of the day...

Yep, as the country threatens to sink below the waves both literally and metaphorically, our liege in waiting, Bonehead Prince Charlie, boldly stepped into the breach this week to announce he was launching a new campaign—to save the red squirrel.

Who said the royals were out of touch, eh? It's that kind of forensic and searing insight coupled with compassion for their fellow man—and an abiding fondness for nazi regalia—that make the Windsors such natural leaders.

Don't get me wrong. I like a squirrel as much as the next man, unless the next bloke's Bill Oddie, in which case it's just weird.

The noble Sciurus vulgaris is a much-loved and iconic creature, and in at least one case it's made a valuable contribution to road safety. But should there not be a sense of proportion here?

A week ago the Tories were going to flog off every scrap of woodland this country possessed, but I didn't hear the prince make any clarion cries to action over that. Where would your squirrels have been then, Charlie? Up to their nuts in trouble, that's where.

But the great Ikea—er, I mean forestry—sell-off was yet another policy the Tories were forced to backtrack on this week, going the same way as stealing milk from kiddies, using public funds to pay for a private photographer and scrapping school sports.

Apparently selling off the nation's heritage for a quick buck irked the electorate somewhat ... who'd have thought?

It's when the Tories try to think up new ideas rather than rely on the tried and tested Conservative mainstays of knee-jerk reactionism and bigotry that it all goes wrong for them.

You could hunt poor people with hounds through their back gardens and middle England would applaud you, but don't mess with their forestry. Ironically if the Tories reverted to one of their favourite topics and said they had to get rid of the woodlands because asylum-seekers could hide in them, Kent would be covered in sawdust by now.

Perhaps learning from this, Iain Duncan Smith reverted to type this week and vowed to crack down on the "workshy" as part of his swingeing welfare cuts.

It takes some chutzpah to put hundreds of thousands of people out of work then blame them for not having a job. But then honesty and this coalition go together like the royals and animal welfare—they're flexible concepts.

They dwell in the moral hinterland which simultaneously allows Prince Charles to weep for the plight of the red squirrel and then decry the fact that he and his inbred offspring aren't allowed to get togged up and rip foxes to shreds any more.

The same shadowy netherworld of ambiguity allows David Cameron to claim with a straight face that decimating public services and running the country into the ground is a positive thing because it will usher in the Big Society.

In fact you could even say that the same vacuum of integrity means that the Tories are condemning workshy scroungers while spending millions of our money on the coming nuptials of two parasites who never worked a day in their lives.

But of course even the Tories wouldn't be that hypocritical, would they?

as right to kill up 1
"really honestly" believe

In the grip

decided to rule ou
r's smugness and me
ausing a conflagrat.
ng act of self-immo

nting the possibili
and confess all, re
devote the rest of

Supporters of an
unelected despot
were set to
blockade roads and
stage mass
demonstrations
across the country.
The police and army
were
planning
not to
crack
heads but
to join
the
banner-
waving.
And the
papers were
cheering the whole
sorry show. All but
one, anyway

lay
cha
r s
rtm

fel
hir
. be

is
ci

eek
th
pop
ks

bab
lf.

was

hose
not
on

thi

cul

JP Mo
b
a

MONARCHY
All royals are equal, Clegg insists

ssianic tendencies

g at his blatant h
d by the breathtak

tember 11 to the

ight years ago.

this egregious c

of extremism

This month will see thousands of dangerous extremists take to the streets of Britain planning mass demonstrations across the country. Roads will be blocked, traffic paralysed, offensive slogans chanted and banners brandished.

And what are the government planning to do about it? Declaring it a national holiday, that's what. This royal wedding business has got completely out of hand.

Come April 29 we won't be able to move for drunken monarchists garrotting innocent bystanders with lethal lengths of bunting and flapping commemorative tea towels at each other like demented Morris dancers.

Where is the Territorial Support Group when you need it? It should be out there cracking heads—let's face it, some of them are bound to be students.

Listening to the media, or the government, you could be forgiven for thinking that an earth-shattering event of global importance was about to occur which will unite the nation in rapture and end the recession—not the fact that a couple of toffs are getting spliced.

Just about every home news story now has to have a royal wedding "hook." The theft of £36,000 worth of silver from the barracks of the Household Cavalry last week would normally be enough to merit a story in itself, but we are then breathlessly informed that, "at the royal wedding on April 29, the regiment will have a key role."

The Evening Standard, the culprits behind the offending piece, also brayed, no doubt in an attempt to elicit further outrage, that both William and Harry are members of the regiment.

I'm no detective but in that case I would think they merited questioning. Sounds like a stag night prank to me. For most people it's a case of tying the groom up in a public place and putting a traffic cone on their head, but as this is the Windsors you have to up the stakes a bit. And anyway they've already got all the silly hats they need.

They're also hereditary royals and therefore used to stealing what's not theirs and getting away with it—admittedly usually things like countries and whacking great diamonds, but the principle's the same.

Not that there is allowed to be any criticism of the blessed Windsors and their insignificant others in the organs of the fourth estate these days. You'd have more chance trying to get the News of the World to publish a story about phone-hacking.

Typing Kate Middleton's name into the search engine of that well-known arbiter of good taste the Daily Express elicits a mere 448 puff pieces about the "radiant" and "slimline" bride to be. Not to be outdone the Beeb has said that it is sending 550 staff to report on the noxious nuptials. I didn't think they had that many staff left.

Everywhere you look there are gushing eulogies to the couple as if they were some kind of Romeo and Juliet-style pair of star-crossed lovers united against the odds.

The odds in this case presumably being the likelihood that one of them would be too thick to close their mouth when it was raining and drown.

Miles of column inches have been dedicated to swooning hagiographies in the "prince and the pauper" vein. Much is made of the fact that Middleton is a "commoner," by which they mean her parents weren't cousins.

Well, if the privately educated, pampered, soon to be princess Middleton is a commoner, what does that make the rest of us? Feudal serfs?

But what is truly obnoxious is that at a time when the coalition is making millions unemployed and attempting to prevent peaceful, lawful protest against the brutality of their cuts agenda they are urging the country to take to the streets and rejoice in this farcical pantomime.

as right to kill up
"really honestly" believe

The year of

We barely had five minutes' peace after the royal wedding before the fawning and grovelling started up again--this time over charmless old bigot Prince Philip's achievement in reaching 90 without accidentally shooting himself in the head

decided to rule out
r's smugness and me
ausing a conflagrat
ng act of self-immo

nting the possibili
and confess all, re
devote the rest of

"adviser" to JP Mo
after he handed ba

ROYAL FAMILY

Prince Philip and the edited CV

Happy birthday Prince Philip! What started as a teenage correspondence has turned into a life sentence which he has borne with fortitude enlivened by occasional verbal infelicities.

But he had a number of hurdles to overcome, starting with some creative CV editing.

Being born into the Greek royal family was not such a big impediment in itself. The family name was, so the German-Dutch house of Holstein, it was the German-Dutch house of Schleswig-Holstein-Sonderburg-Glücksburg was carefully airbrushed out of the story.

Next to go was his religious affiliation. Her Majesty may be an Anglican who magically transmutes into a Presbyterian when she crosses the border to Scotland, but a Greek Orthodox spouse would complicate the story rather too much.

The Greek and Dutch royal titles also vanished. The Greek bit had become rather academic — his family were but a

Becoming a naturalised British subject was no problem. But what name to adopt? The solution was to adopt Mountbatten — the anglicised name of his maternal grandfather Prince Louis of Battenberg.

His immediate family were bit more difficult. Big sister Margarita was married to a German army officer who had fought the Soviets — not so popular in the immediate post-war solidarity with our Soviet allies.

Sister Theodora was married to the impressively named Berthold Friedrich Wilhelm Ernst August Heinrich Karl, Margrave of Baden.

Sister Cecile is best glossed over, having married her first cousin Georg Donatus, Hereditary Grand Duke of Hesse. They both joined the Nazi Party.

Sophie was equally embarrassing. She married Prince Christoph Ernst August of Hesse — an SS officer, Luftwaffe major, aide to Himmler and intelligence chief to Hermann Goering.

He was killed in the invasion of Italy — but he could not go to the wedding. Nor was it thought polite to invite the sisters. Maybe they were sent a piece of the wedding cake as consolation.

NICK WRIGHT

tember 11 to the

ight years ago.

this egregious c

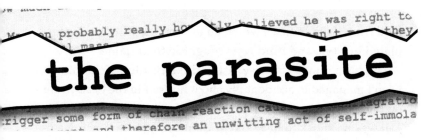

the parasite

trigger some form of chain reaction ca... ...gratio ... ...therefore an unwitting act of self-immola...

Have I missed a trick and there's suddenly a new Chinese year? Because by any reasonable estimation 2011 can only be the year of the parasite.

We've had the farcically sycophantic slavering about the royal nuptials and Lizzy Brit on her jaunt to the Emerald Isle to patronise the locals.

Even bloody Fergie has cropped up again on US chat shows to whine that she looks in the mirror and thinks she's useless … presumably waiting vainly for someone to contradict her.

And now we're apparently supposed to get all dewy-eyed and patriotic because that old bigot the Duke of Edinburgh has managed to stay alive to be 90.

It was the same with the Queen Mother. "Ooh, isn't she marvellous!" they fawned as they watched this cadaverous old crone toddle from one hand-out to the next.

Well, quite frankly, no she wasn't. She was a small-minded bully and arrogant bigot with an overblown sense of entitlement completely at odds with her actual worth.

If anyone had never done a tap in their lives and had spent the majority of it swanning around in a perfume-scented bubble of taxpayer-funded luxury they'd probably make it to 90 too.

Unfortunately the overwhelming majority of the population do not have this pampered existence and have to work themselves into an early grave only to see the bulk of their money bled from them in taxes which go to fund the Windsors' gold-plated lifestyle and fund wars fought in their name.

The only minor surprise at the duke turning 90 is that he hasn't managed to accidentally shoot himself in the head while on one of his numerous safaris in the Highlands.

It was no shock to hear David Cameron give an unctuously lickspittle eulogy to the royal hanger-on in Parliament this week, urging MPs to support plans for "a humble address to be presented to her majesty" on the occasion.

He's related to them somewhere down the line, after all.

Cameron described Phil the Greek as a "remarkable man" who "defended his nation in time of war"—yes, but which nation?

He was "a man who has given his time and effort and passion to so many great causes," Cameron gushed.

Presumably that was a reference to the duke juggling his penchant for maiming small animals with chairing the World Wildlife Fund. He's like the anti-Noah.

Cameron also made much of his great work in the Commonwealth and around the world.

I don't know if you can call abusing the foreigners "work" exactly. But, to give him his due, Philip's dedicated to it. He's called the Chinese slitty-eyed, the Scots alcoholics, Hungarians pot-bellied and the natives of Papua New Guinea cannibals. He also mocked the unemployed for complaining about not having jobs during the 1981 recession.

When it comes to global diplomacy he's in a league of two rivalled only by Silvio Berlusconi and the recently relegated Bernard Manning.

In fact the only MP with any guts was Labour backbencher Paul Flynn who blasted Cameron's sycophancy and said his proposed "humble address" demeaned Parliament.

"Are the royal family superior beings to the rest of us? Are we inferior beings to them?" he queried. "That was the feeling of the house seven centuries ago when we accepted the rules under which we speak now."

It's a pity his party leader didn't see fit to take such a principled stand. If anything Ed Miliband's witterings were more obsequious than Cameron's.

The Labour leader trumpeted that "the duke is a reminder to us all of the unique spirit of public service which the monarchy discharges to the British people at home and abroad.

"His unique turn of phrase has become a much-loved feature of modern British life," he added.

Well, so's the Daily Mail in many places, but it's still sexist, racist, homophobic and borderline fascist.

Bahrain

What's the problem with holding a grand prix in a country whose government is beating, shooting and torturing pro-democracy protesters? Nothing, according to F1 chief Bernie Ecclestone and a disgraced former Met copper working for, er, the Bahraini regime

FORMULA ONE: POLITICS IN SPORT

'Only Bahrain can cancel grand prix'

F1 chief Ecclestone says any decision down to locals

MIDDLE EAST

Ex-Met chief slammed over F1 letter

Shamed former cop tells teams Bahrain is 'safer than London'

This column usually steers well clear of the subject of sport—not for it the minute discussion of the relative merits of the 4-4-2 versus 4-3-3 formations or whether league or union is the apogee of the game.

There are far too many others spouting rubbish and behaving appallingly without having to trawl through the subliterate tweeting of footie philosophers or the conspiracy theories of messrs Dalglish, Mancini and Ferguson et al.

In fact even the use of the term "sport" is disputable in some instances. Legendary darts commentator Sid Waddell did indeed once state: "Jocky Wilson, what an athlete," but he also memorably described another player as having "eyes like a pterodactyl with contact lenses."

Waddell is a genius—intentionally or not—of the spoken word. Many others attached even peripherally to the sporting world are not.

The main reason this column doesn't do sport is because it is a field of which it has little knowledge.

That however hasn't stopped senior figures in the sporting world from weighing in with spectacularly ill-judged and crass opinions on the issues of the day in recent times, so here goes...

They say that sport and politics should not mix, but it would appear no-one told Bernie Ecclestone, the FIA or the Bahraini regime and their willing shills this.

Yes, as democratic protesters are being beaten, shot, tear-gassed, imprisoned and tortured in ever increasing numbers the big concern of the day appears to be whether a bunch of spoiled, pampered multimillionaires can drive really fast in their overblown go-karts around a track.

They don't even go anywhere. Just round and round in circles, a bit like the regime's pledges to improve its human rights record after massacring protesters during the Arab spring.

At the weekend Ecclestone, the diminutive doyen of motor racing, stated: "Everybody's happy. We haven't got any problems."

Of course he's happy and doesn't have any problems, he's a sodding billionaire.

"It's a problem being discussed by the media. They don't have any idea what's going on. That's the problem."

So, not a bunch of blood-soaked despots murdering their own people then? "There's nothing happening. I know people who live there and it's all very quiet and peaceful." Yes, Bernie, and your daughters are the shy retiring types.

In a report published this week, Amnesty said that abuses continue unabated in Bahrain and warned that going ahead with the grand prix would send a message to the regime that it was acceptable to continue its abuses.

Still, Ecclestone must be used to cosying up to human rights abusers and war criminals by now. A few years ago he gave Tony Blair so much money he got a knighthood.

But it wasn't just Ecclestone. Former England Under-21s manager and apparently self-styled PR guy for tyrannical autocratic regimes Peter Taylor also put his mouth where his money is and, showing the tact and forethought for which footballers are renowned, declared the Bahrain Grand Prix should go ahead.

Taylor, who took over as coach of Bahrain's national football team in July and therefore may have a vested interest in whether his next cheque gets signed, said he could not see "any point" in calling the grand prix off.

"There are problems here but I also fear more is made of them than they are (sic)," he shilled. "Personally I haven't witnessed many protests."

You'll notice the use of the word "many" there. A somewhat subjective term.

Many, many people have been killed and tortured by the regime and its thugs, probably using weapons sold to them by UK plc, but to former Met commander John Yates it's a case of "move along, nothing to see here."

He felt safer there than in London, he said, although that may have been because there was a strong possibility he would be nicked for corruption while in Blighty.

Ecclestone hinted this week at a new grand prix to take place in Africa. Given his track record my money's on Libya or the Democratic Republic of Congo. There's nothing going on there, is there?

Queen kills

Diamond jubilee
celebrations had
barely got into
first gear when
the nation was
sent reeling by
revelations that
Elizabeth Windsor
had the blood of
innocent seabirds
on her hands--
not that you'd
know it from the
yellow press or our
             toadying
             politicians

as right to kill up
"really honestly" believe

decided to rule ou
r's smugness and me
ausing a conflagrat
ng act of self-immo

nting the possibili
and confess all, re
devote the rest of

"adviser" to JP Mo
s after he handed b

e stand at an inqu
e Hague, he took a
Lansdowne Partner

absolutely everyor

ssianic tendencies

g at his blatant h
d by the breathtak

tember 11 to the

ght years ago.

this egregious c

probably really ho ... tly believed he was right to ... sn't ... they ... mas ...

cormorants

trigger some form of chain reaction cau ... agratio ... and therefore an unwitting act of self-immola

QUEEN KILLS CORMORANTS—that's the headline that the yellow media is too scared to run this week, but it's true.

Oh yes, not content with having sole rights to our swans—and a major share in the national corgi stockpile—it emerged this week that now she wants to kill off our sea-bound wildlife.

The craven running dogs of the monarchist, crypto-fascist, lickspittle press are trying to bury this story for reasons too chilling to go into here but almost certainly connected with the Masons, Jack the Ripper and a hushed-up incident involving Prince Albert and a frisky otter. Well, this column will not be gagged!

You see they hate wildlife, the Windsors. Loathe and despise nature in all its myriad forms. If they can't eat it they'll kill it anyway, just for the fun of it. They'll kill us too if they get the chance which is why this must be stopped now.

So insidious, so villainous, so inutterably evil is this plot that it fair makes one shudder to contemplate it.

Not content with their usual method of exterminating wildlife—telling Prince Philip it's an endangered species and standing well back or letting Prince Charles tear it to pieces with hounds—they have gone one further.

Rather than having the blood of the poor innocent creatures on their own bejewelled hands for all to see they have hatched a plot worthy of Mephistopheles himself.

Namely biding their time until such time as the great she-beast had been on the throne for three score years and then making you, and your children, do it for her.

Yes, according to a shocking report—the Marine Conservation Society's annual litter survey—our beaches are becoming festooned with the rotting remnants of bunting and balloons, the festering flotsam and jetsam of the jubilee celebrations.

This year, 2012, levels have soared with an almost 10 per cent rise in the number of balloons discarded as so much detritus on our golden sands.

The small creatures so despised by the crown become entangled, some even throttled or choked, on these blaggardly bladders, these diminutive dirigibles.

In a ghastly irony they will spend the last moments of their fleeting lives gazing through dimming eyes at a monstrous grinning visage of their nemesis, Elizabeth Windsor.

I'm not saying the citizens of this country shouldn't have their jubilee parties ... I'm just saying every time they do a puffin dies.

And what are our elected representatives doing about it? Nothing, nada, not a jot. Because the monarchy is an "institution" we're told. Admittedly a few of them should be in one, but come off it.

The MPs were falling all over each other in a bid to out-genuflect and ingratiate themselves with Liz and Phil when they turned up in Parliament this week. Curiously every one of them studiously ignored the glaring fact that if her ancestors had had their way what laughably passes for democracy in this country wouldn't exist and they'd all be out of a job.

Labour were just as bad as the Tories, with Ed Miliband apparently so excited he couldn't find the right queue to join for the traditional forelock tugging.

It was a "wonderful, memorable occasion" for people to "pay tribute to the extraordinary service of Her Majesty," he smarmed. "Everybody here will remember this occasion for the rest of their lives."

And, thanks to the Tories and invertebrate Lib Dems, those lives will probably be a good deal shorter as of this week.

The servile simpering that greeted the royals was in stark contrast to the treatment meted out to a real British institution in the Commons that very day—the NHS.

Setting aside all notions of sanity and the advice of anyone with any knowledge on the subject the Tories finally succeeded in ringing the death knell for public health care and then cheerfully quaffed champagne with the nobs.

Sick doesn't cover it.

Tucking in

In case the
endless--
and extremely
expensive--jubilee
celebrations
weren't offensive
enough the Queen
decided to invite
some of the world's
worst despots to
a lavish Windsor
Castle lunch and
an even more
glittering Buck
House dinner.
With the taxpayer
picking up the
bill, naturally

ROYALS

Fury as Queen plans dinner with despots

s right to kill up 1
"really honestly" believe

decided to rule out
r's smugness and me
ausing a conflagrat
ng act of self-immo

nting the possibili
and confess all, re
devote the rest of

"adviser" to JP Mo
s after he handed b

he stand at an inqu
he Hague, he took a
d Lansdowne Partner

absolutely everyor

ssianic tendencies

tember 11 to the 1

ight years ago.

this egregious c

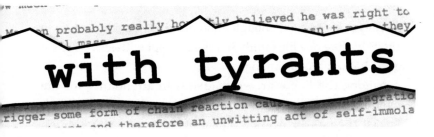

with tyrants

They say blood is thicker than water, and this week for the umpteenth time it was proved that if it's blue it's more viscous still. It's a much-played parlour game—who would you invite to your ideal dinner party? In Lizzy Brit's case it seems to be anyone up to the oxters in gore.

Yep, not content with bleeding the country dry and boring the arse off the nation with her interminable jubilee shenanigans, our titular head of state decided to wine and dine some of the worst despots on the planet.

There were the crown heads of Brunei, Bahrain, Saudi Arabia and Qatar—all of whom have presided over bloody slaughters of their own civilians in the last 12 months. I think King Hussein of Jordan's invite must have got lost in the post...

Still, what's a bit of extra-judicial murder and torture between friends?

I can just imagine the wistful look in Phil the Greek's eyes. "We used to be able to do that in the good old days (sigh). Now the only things we can shoot are pheasants. It's just not the bloody same." It will be interesting to see what mots justes he comes up with for the occasion. "Ah, good you've brought your own tea towel because you're doing the washing up!"

The choice of Windsor Castle was ironically appropriate as a venue for the slap-up lunch as it's wont to burst into flames on almost as regular a basis as these murderous tyrants' countries.

They just can't get enough of bloodthirsty psychopaths can they? It's like one big family reunion, except with less criticism and character assassination.

Among the home-grown parasites in attendance for the evening shindig at Buck House were—in keeping with the fascist theme—Princess Michael of Kent, who this column is reliably informed entertained the guests with a rousing rendition of that old English standard My Old Man's an Obergruppenführer.

And of course that legendary ligger Airmiles Andy also made an appearance. Still at least it probably cost us fractionally less to get the freeloading scumbag to Buck House than it usually does to jet him around the globe to press the flesh with murderous tyrants and flog them stuff.

With this Who's Who of human rights abusers swanning around London it was left to Alistair Darling to take a stand ... by condemning the decision to rescind Fred the Shred Goodwin's knighthood as it brought the honours system into disrepute!

Nice to see the former chancellor taking such a principled stance against the avarice of the banking industry.

Now the churlish might suggest that it would take more than stripping a gong from a chancer who should be in jail to bring an archaic imperialist system based on slavery, subjugation and slaughter into disrepute.

They gave one to Jeffrey Archer, for God's sake. If that's not scraping the bottom of the barrel, I don't know what is.

Darling told the Commons public administration committee that he did "not carry a particular flag" for Goodwin. He does have his name scratched on his pencil case though.

The whole episode—removing the honour—had "backfired" with the public, he claimed, blatantly ignoring the fact that what "backfired" was the multibillion-pound bailouts for the banks which went straight into fat cats' pockets as bonuses and which we're still bloody paying for.

Still, at least we've got the Olympic torch coming. Nothing controversial about that ... apart, that is, from that whole thing having been invented as a propaganda exercise by the nazis...

David Beckham and Boris Johnson might as well have been wearing KKK outfits—they have a thing about burning symbols too.

You can dress it up with as many Grecian "priestesses" in togas as you want. It's still the athletic equivalent of Triumph of the Will. Enjoy!

as right to kill up
"really honestly" believe

Immaculate

Revisionism all
round as Madonna,
in the great
British tradition,
airbrushed
the royal
family's nazi
leanings out of
history while,
confronted
with an Occupy
protest on the
doorstep of St
Paul's, the Church
of England insisted
it had always been
Christian policy
to invite the
money changers into
the temple

decided to rule out
r's smugness and men
ausing a conflagrati
ng act of self-immo

Fascist fashion

WE (18)
Directed by Madonna
☆☆☆☆☆

he stand at an inqu
he Hague, he took a
d Lansdowne Partner

absolutely everyor

ssianic tendencies

OCCUPYLSX
Protesters face eviction bid
Cathedral bosses and councillors launch legal action to kick out anti-greed occupation

at his blatant h

ight years ago.

this egregious c

correction

I t was reported this week that a playwright has taken the unusual step of scrapping his own work—a stage drama drawing on the events of World War II—after the body that commissioned it decided he was not allowed to mention the nazis, the Jews or the invasion of Poland.

Now it could be said that penning an opus about the 1939-45 war without at least one of those elements appearing, even fleetingly, would be rather tricky. In fact it would be akin to attempting to write a definitive biography of Robert Maxwell without the words crook, pensions and overboard.

The Halloween play was originally approved to be performed as part of "ghost tours" at Pendennis Castle, in Falmouth, Cornwall, over four nights for an "adults-only" audience, with scenes showcasing different periods in the Tudor castle's history, including its second world war gun batteries.

According to the scribe himself, the reason given by English Heritage, the august organisation in question, for its frankly baffling decision was apparently that it was concerned that the mention of the Third Reich, the semitic race and/or the birthplace of a former pope might "offend people."

Am I the only one who thinks that failure to mention the fight against fascism and the murder of six million Jews might also get a few backs up...

Someone with no such qualms regarding self-censorship and blatant revisionism, however, is Madonna.

Yes, the Material Girl has—in keeping with her latest incarnation as a member of the landed gentry—entered into that noble British tradition of completely airbrushing out of history the fact that our royals were about as pally with Hitler as you could get without actually being Eva Braun.

Her new hagiographical biopic of Wallis Simpson, W.E., it has been noted, not so much skirts around but veers violently away from any suggestion that La Simpson and her other half Edward VIII were—how shall we put it?—somewhat rose-tinted in their view of the Führer and his project.

About all she didn't do was turn up with pom-poms and shout "Give me an 'A'…" What's a holocaust or two between friends, eh?

The ex-Mrs Ritchie, showing that she shared her erstwhile spouse's eye for period detail, said she found no "empirical evidence" that Simpson was a nazi sympathiser.

Well thank you, pop's answer to Simon Schama. No doubt she employed the same forensic level of research she did when cobbling together Evita, which now I come to think of it also involved reinventing a dodgy old fascist.

At this juncture it's important to note that there is absolutely no truth in the rumour doing the rounds that David Cameron is to appoint Madonna as his new PR guru.

Although this column understands there is a script in the pipeline for a bold reimagining of the life of a certain grocer's daughter from Grantham which tells the hitherto undocumented story of how she discovered the Falklands and saved Arthur Scargill from a pit disaster by digging him out with her bare hands.

When it comes to rewriting the traditional version of events, however, Madge is a mere amateur. There is only one true contender to the crown this week—the Anglicans.

Yes, the C of E—with the honourable exception of Canon Giles Fraser—in cahoots with the London Corporation, has this week decided on a radical reinterpretation of the parable of Jesus casting the money lenders out of the temple.

At the same time as it was revealed that grasping company directors trousered average pay rises of 49 per cent last year the church showed in no uncertain terms where its sympathies lie.

The new version appears to be "It's true Jesus said: 'My house shall be called the house of prayer; but ye have made it a den of thieves,' but ... if you mess with our cash flow and stop those wealthy tourists coming you'll get your head stoved in."

s right to kill up 1
"really honestly" believe

Black and

lay
cha
r s
rtm

fel
hin
be

ls i
ici

Our human rights
watchdog claimed
the emptiest of
legal victories
when the British
National Party
bowed to its demand
to allow non-white
members. Form an
orderly queue...

decided to rule out
r's smugness and me:
ausing a conflagrat:
ng act of self-immo

nting the possibili
and confess all, re
devote the rest of

"adviser" to JP Mo:
s after he handed b:

MEMBERSHIP RIGHTS ROW
Watchdog takes BNP to court

po
ks

bab
lf.

vas

hose
not
on

thi

cul

l Lansdowne Partner

absolutely everyor

ssianic tendencies

g at his blatant h
d by the breathtak

tember 11 to the]

ight years ago.

this egregious c

white power?

So the Equality and Human Rights Commission is claiming victory in its crusade to force the BNP to "consider" allowing non-white members to join. Hmm...

Surely I'm not the only one who sees a gaping hole in the logic and a fairly gigantic pachyderm trying to look nonchalant in the corner of the room here.

Just how many Muslims or black people do you think would want to join a party consisting entirely of white, knuckle-dragging racists?

"Well, I don't agree with the whole 'white power, ethnic minorities are inferior' shtick, but their karaoke nights are fantastic!"

But no, in the face of all rational thought the EHRC and its bold helmsman Trevor Phillips are trumpeting this as a landmark victory.

It has been argued that anything that drags the BNP through the courts and highlights its intolerance is worthwhile and generally I would agree.

But what exactly has this achieved? Absolutely nothing positive, I would argue. In fact bringing the case in the first place was such an idiotic premise it makes the Flat Earth Society appear rational and well-balanced. It seemed more calculated to make headlines than to benefit anyone else.

Counsel for the commission Robin Allen QC said Nick Griffin—the boss bootboy or chief pointy-head or whatever the hell he calls himself these days—had agreed to present party members with a revised constitution at the BNP general meeting next month.

Well, I'm sure Griffin will put this proposal to his party members in a reasoned and fair manner and of course he wouldn't use the opportunity to rabble-rouse about how they are being victimised by a nanny state and stir up outrage against "bleeding-heart liberals coming in here and messing with our constitution."

Half his members probably didn't even know there was a constitution except "we hate black people" scrawled on a bus stop somewhere in Essex.

The BNP apparently agreed to use "all reasonable endeavours" to revise its constitution so it did not discriminate.

Oh well, that's all right then. First you take the word of a known nazi and liar and then you don't even get a solemn promise in the first place.

I shudder to think what "all reasonable endeavours" means to these thugs. Equal opportunity lynchings?

The only "good" thing about the BNP is that it does exactly what it says on the tin, namely being obviously bigoted and racist, and that this is so abhorrent to all right-minded people that they would rather cut off their arm than join or vote for it.

In one fell swoop the EHRC has gifted BNP members a wonderful get-out, by allowing it to say: "Well, it's not our fault if no ethnic minorities want to join." It also allows them to play the martyr.

Indeed no sooner had the EHRC press release landed on my desk than the BNP were branding this a "Marxist plot." Nice one!

So now it's possible for anyone to join the BNP. Well, it's "possible" for anyone to join a doomsday cult and take part in synchronised suicide, but that doesn't mean it's a good idea or something that should be seriously considered.

The EHRC has totally missed the point with this case—the issue surrounding the BNP is not that it won't let black or Asian people join, it's that it exists at all.

hearing I had reluctantly decided to rule

sheer enormity of Blair's smugness and me

form of chain reaction causing a conflagrati

and therefore an unwitting act of self-immo

did was try to link September 11 to the Ir

cular claim didn't hold water eight years a

evidence to support this egregious claim be

were carried out mainly by

urprise, surprise. Tony Blair thinks he wa
illion people in an illegal war because he
e was right.

ell, that was worth £250k of public money
nows how much in inquiry salaries, wasn't

arles Manson probably really honestly bel:
every egomania   derer in

Rogue Bosses &
Greedy Swine

y'll probably be entitled "How to shaft ab
e yourself."

Blair was always going to allow his messi;
—yet again.

s right to kill up
"really honestly" believe

Pitbulls in

After years of
campaigning
Britain finally
gave official
recognition to
International
Workers Memorial
Day. But
that was
small
consolation
to tens of
thousands
of asbestos
sufferers
still fighting for
compensation or to
the future victims
of Tory safety cuts

decided to rule out
r's smugness and me
ausing a conflagrat.
ng act of self-immo

nting the possibili
and confess all, re
devote the rest of

60,000 MORE TO DIE OF ASBESTOS

Bosses' waiting game could leave a total of 90,000 without justice

ne Hague, he took
d Lansdowne Partner

absolutely everyor

ssianic tendencies

£2m payouts show deadly risk

d by the breathtak

tember 11 to the

ight years ago.

this egregious c

the nursery

As we prepare to mark Workers Memorial Day on Wednesday it is perhaps instructive to cast an eye over the track record of the three main parties on this most important of issues.

Not one of them has made any mention of this country's shameful record on workplace safety in their luridly designed manifestos or, more tellingly, what they propose to do to rectify the situation.

A revolving-door policy in the courts allows firms such as Corus, Biffa and their odious ilk to continue to act with all the morality of a rabid rottweiler in a kindergarten.

But at least you could argue that a rottweiler doesn't know any better. These murderous firms know exactly what they are doing—they just don't care.

An estimated 50,000 workers lose their lives each year due to the cynical scrimping and cost-cutting of these grasping firms which, for a slight increase in profits, risk employees' lives on a daily basis.

Perhaps the most villainous example of this is still having repercussions today. The use of asbestos as a cheap alternative building material was rife in this country years after the dangers were known. Workers were effectively handed death sentences on a scale which would make a Texas judge blush. The dangers were known by the firms and by the government of the day, but not by the workers.

I interviewed a mesothelioma sufferer from Bradford a few years ago and he recounted how he and his colleagues had actually questioned the safety of the new wonder material in the 1960s.

A shop steward had asked for safety equipment but was told that asbestos was absolutely safe. Laggers were mixing the stuff and applying it with their bare hands. Thousands of workers have or will die in excruciating pain from asbestos-related cancers due to callous employers.

And now these same employers with their battery of pernicious insurers are attempting to screw them out of compensation. This they are doing with the active connivance of the House of Lords and the government.

Asbestos is only one, albeit major, cause of workplace death and illness. Each year hundreds die in preventable accidents in the workplace.

Biffa alone has been prosecuted and fined 16 times by the Health and Safety Executive in the last 10 years for negligent behaviour leading to fatalities and injuries on its sites. Corus has a similarly deplorable record of maiming and killing its workers and was prosecuted three times in one month by the HSE.

To paraphrase Oscar Wilde, to lose one worker is a tragedy, to lose three (or more) is criminal. And what do our elected representatives do about this? Oh, there's plenty of hand-wringing when the cameras are rolling on the election trail, but behind the scenes they do damn all.

Even on the self-serving level that they all seem to be operating on, this is potentially hundreds of thousands of votes. You'd think that would worry someone, wouldn't you?

In fact the Tories, not content with having flogged off most of the national industries and attempting to decimate the public sector, now want to privatise health and safety inspections and let firms self-regulate.

It takes a certain sort of genius to look at a situation and say: "Hmm. Thousands of people dying each year from preventable accidents—how can we make it worse?"

But of course there is absolutely no connection between the fact that this will benefit big business and that the Tory Party is almost exclusively bankrolled by, er, big business.

No connection at all … and you would be a fool and a pinko lefty to make one.

as right to kill up 1
"really honestly" believed

Oilier than

BP found itself
renamed Bayou
Polluter as
the stricken
Deepwater
Horizon rig
continued to
gush oil into the
Gulf of Mexico--but
the disaster
didn't do any
immediate
damage to its
share price or
its slippery
            chief
            exec

US DISASTER
Search halted
for survivors
11 workers still missing after oil rig explosion

US
Gulf oil spill begins
to ooze ashore
Obama puts new drilling on hold as Washington investigates explosion

**New plan as top
kill proves useless**

decided to rule out
r's smugness and men
ausing a conflagrat:
lf-imno
re
of

"adviser" to JP Mo:
s after he handed b;

absolutely everyor

ssianic tendencies

g at his blatant h
d by the breathtak

tember 11 to the 1

ght years ago.

this egregious c

a Tory MP

The latest attempt at environmental armageddon unleashed on an unsuspecting world has seen British Petroleum turn a large proportion of the Gulf of Mexico into a toxic soup which will decimate the local flora and fauna for years to come. Still, it's only the planet, isn't it?

What exactly goes on in the heads of these oil company execs and their avaricious shareholders, other than how much can we wreck the planet and plunder its natural resources and still be alive to make money?

I only ask because following the most horrific oil pollution incident in recent years nobody seems particularly keen to disinvest in BP, or Bayou Polluter as it is being jocularly titled by members of its own staff.

In fact I would go as far as to say there are probably quite a lot of stockbrokers and their verminous ilk thinking: "Hmm, share prices sinking like an oil-lathered cormorant—good time to buy!" You have to be of a particularly warped mindset to see an ecological disaster on a massive scale and think: "I could make a few bob out of that!"

The main source of bemusement for me is that everyone seems so surprised that this happened. It was never going to go well, was it? When you put the names BP and Halliburton together in any context someone somewhere was always going to get shafted—it's just that it's usually Iraqis and to all intents and purposes they don't count.

Yep, BP with the assistance of the smarmiest guys in the room put their heads together and produced the biggest oil slick in US history. More devastating even than Exxon Valdez.

BP and the US government are desperately trying to down-play the damage of course, claiming that only 5,000 barrels of oil a day are vomiting into the sea.

Environmental experts put that figure at closer to 25,000-30,000 barrels a day. That would create enough Brylcreem to keep the entire Republican Party going for a year.

BP chief exec Tony Hayward, who took over from former boss John Browne who ironically had to stand down after some unpleasantness in the US himself, has described the amount of oil haemorrhaging out of the busted pipe as minuscule in proportion to the volume of the Gulf of Mexico.

This prompted Ian Macdonald, a biological oceanographer at Florida State University, to ask the wonderful question: "This Tiny (sic) Hayward, is he a lord or a duke or a knight or something?", adding with scathing irony: "I reckon he must be very important because every time he appears on our television screens he produces the most astonishing insights. I'm a biological oceanographer and I've never heard it explained like that before."

And how did BP respond to this devastating incident? First it tried to lower a big perspex dome over the leak. It didn't work but at least it'll give Sting and Bono somewhere to stage their inevitable benefit gig.

Then it decided to deal with a massive pollution leak by stuffing the hole full of old golf balls and rubbish.

Now call me a dangerous subversive if you wish but would it not be a good idea BEFORE we let these vandals start raping the planet to find out if they know what to do in case of a cock-up?

It's like letting someone perform open-heart surgery and then watching with interest at the attempt to stem the bleeding by stuffing the cavity full of old crisp packets, chewing gum and rubber gloves.

Although, with the Tories' plans for the NHS, it's probably only a matter of time.

as right to kill up 1
"really honestly" believe

Fishing for

decided to rule out
r's smugness and mer
ausing a conflagrat:
ng act of self-immo

The Revenue named
and shamed its
20 most wanted
tax-dodgers but
a few faces were
strangely absent
from the rogues'
gallery--like the
government's own
spending
adviser
Sir
Philip
Green

nting the possibili
and confess all, re
devote the rest of

"adviser" to JP Mo:
s after he handed b;

EVASION SEARCH

HMRC names most wanted tax dodgers

But no action on tax-avoiding corporations

absolutely everyor

ssianic tendencies

g at his blatant h
d by the breathtak

otember 11 to the 1

ght years ago.

this egregious c

minnows

This week the world of politics has outdone itself by going to such extremes of lunacy that it has almost transcended satire. Almost.

The Treasury and HM Revenue and Customs this week took the unusual step of naming and shaming tax-dodgers in an FBI-style 10 most wanted list. Twenty wanted fraudsters, avoiders and evaders were outed and had their mugshots posted on the web.

Exchequer Secretary David Gauke said: "These criminals have collectively cost the taxpayer over £765 million and HMRC will pursue them relentlessly. We hope that publishing their pictures in this way will enable members of the public to contribute to the effort to catch them."

Anyone perusing the rogues' gallery even perfunctorily may have got a nagging feeling that something wasn't quite right, however. As so often in such matters, it wasn't who was on the list, but who wasn't.

Obviously this was one of those unfortunate oversights and in no way a cynical exercise in manipulation in a bid to con the public into thinking that they actually gave a toss about tax-dodging.

Well, never let it be said that this column does not have a sense of civic duty … so allow it to provide a corrective.

The address of Vodafone headquarters is Vodafone House, The Connection, Newbury, Berkshire RG14 2FN.

While those fine upstanding bankers Goldman Sachs can be found at Peterborough Court, 133 Fleet Street, London EC4A 2BB. Vodafone alone apparently avoided paying £4.6 billion following a sweetheart deal with those rigorous types at HMRC. Goldman Sachs ducked paying out £10m in interest on its tax bill.

Another individual who inexplicably does not get a mention is Top Shop fat cat Sir Philip Green, who you will no doubt recall is coincidentally employed as a government spending adviser.

Green is accused of having avoided around £300m in personal taxation by putting everything in his wife's name. He may be slightly more difficult to track down, but if you hang around Downing Street long enough he's bound to turn up.

Even the most numerically challenged can probably see that the almost FIVE BILLION avoided by just these three is considerably more than the £765m that the government is "relentlessly" pursuing.

But then it wouldn't be like this shower to highlight comparative minnows while conveniently turning a blind eye to a whole pod of sodding big whales, would it?

That's kind of like holding a war crimes inquiry and not prosecuting those in power at the time. Oh...

Interestingly most of those named appear to have made their ill-gotten gains via the illegal tobacco market—Ken Clarke obviously doesn't like the competition.

Meanwhile, not to be outdone, the DWP went swinging into action—actually I wish I hadn't typed that. I now have a mental image of Chris Grayling lasciviously rummaging for a car key in a punch bowl—by appointing the director of a firm up to its oxters in blacklisting trade union health and safety reps to the Health and Safety Executive board.

Howard Shiplee is not only an executive director of Laing O'Rourke but was also previously employed by Amec and Carillion—an unholy trinity if ever there was one.

What could possibly go wrong there? It's like appointing Genghis Khan as a roving ambassador, putting the Countess of Báthory in charge of the blood bank, or Andrew Lansley in charge of the NHS.

And speaking of the NHS and tax-dodging freeloaders, it emerged this week that Phil the Greek is back in hospital again. If he was one of the Windsors' beloved horses he'd have been shot by now. He is suffering, we are informed, from a recurrence of his troublesome bladder infection.

Hardly surprising—he's been taking the piss for years.

as right to kill up 1
"really honestly" belleve

Schlock'n'

It was hard to say
what was strangest
about Nick
Buckles's grilling
at the
hands of
MPs--
G4S's
brass
neck in
demanding
payment
for the Olympic
security shambles,
revelations it
has its own soft-
rock corporate
anthem, or the
chief executive's
extraordinary
coiffure

decided to rule out
r's smugness and mer
ausing a conflagrat:
ng act of self-immo

nting the possibili
confess all, re
e rest of

G4S Private-sector pratfall
The Olympics debacle should end wasteful
outsourcing, says MICHAEL MEACHER: P8

SHAMBOLIC G4S STILL WANTS £57 MILLION
MPs left astonished as chief exec admits 'we messed up'

e Hague, he
d Lansdowne

absolutely

ssianic tendencies

g at his blatant h
d by the breathtak

tember 11 to the 1

ight years ago.

this egregious c

lay
cha
r s
rtm

fel
hir
. be

is r
ici.

eek
th
pop
ks

bab
lf.

vas

hose
not
on

thi

icul

roll star

It's the question that has dogged humanity throughout history—what do you give to the sprawling global multi-national that has everything?

Well apparently a soft-rock corporate anthem, if private security's answer to the Keystone Kops—G4S—is anything to go by.

Yes, perhaps the most bizarre facts to emerge from the grilling of G4S chief executive Nick Buckles by MPs this week over the Olympics fiasco—if you discount the fact that the head of a firm which forcibly restrains asylum-seekers is called Buckles—were the titbits that the firm employs more people than the population of Luxembourg and has its own flag and anthem.

Corporate entities have regularly been described as psychopaths and it is common knowledge that they effectively run the world, but G4S seems to have taken it one step further and actually thinks it's a country.

You'd think it'd be able to find a few thousand staff to cover the Games then, wouldn't you?

But then those refugees and inmates at private jails and immigration detention centres don't just beat themselves up. It is a time-consuming and labour-intensive business.

And when you're brutalising people what you need is a good, rousing rock soundtrack to keep morale up and remind you what underappreciated paragons of virtue you are.

G4S: Securing Your World, a soft-rock abomination in a country-tinged style, was apparently cowritten and performed by Texan musician Jon Christopher Davis.

Imagine Jon Bon Jovi vomiting into a bucket while brandishing the Stars and Stripes and you get the gist.

The opus includes such empowering and inspiring lyrics as "because the enemy prowls, wanting to attack/But we're on the wall, we've got your back."

And the buttock-clenchingly awful "G4S! Protecting the world. G4S! So dreams can unfurl." Do you get the impression he was struggling to get a rhyme there? Flags unfurl, dreams don't.

But the sheer bombastic majesty of the following stanza knocks the others into a cocked hat. "Our mission is to maintain the peace/But make no mistake we'll face the beast/We'll back him down and make him run/We'll never leave our post 'til (sic) the job is done."

Or, as recent events have illustrated so amply, not even bother to turn up in the first place.

The second most outlandish element of the committee hearing was Buckles's appearance. He seemed to have had himself entirely laminated, including his hair, which has to be 90 per cent polyester.

And what about that hair? Coupled with the day-glo tan he looked like David Dickinson at a Bay City Rollers reunion. Or Tory MP Michael Fabricant if he'd accidentally put his rug through a dark wash.

In fact, if Fabricant had been in that committee room the effect would have been akin to a Van de Graaff generator.

Such was the pyrotechnic nature of the hearing he should probably have had a fire extinguisher and a bucket of sand close to hand.

But it would be churlish merely to deride Buckles for his sartorial and tonsorial choices, especially when there's so much else to deride him for.

With a straight face he told the committee that the firm still intended to claim £57 million in management fees for a contract it screwed up so spectacularly it made the Tories look almost competent. Or it would have done if they hadn't handed it the contract in the first place.

And then of course there are those other contracts for privatising the police and the military, which are particularly poetic because it's the army and the cops who are having to bail them out. G4S: "Protecting its profits."

Take That,

s right to kill up 1
"really honestly" believes

David Cameron was
quick to jump on
the condemnation
bandwagon when
comedian Jimmy Carr
was caught using
an offshore tax
shelter--but he had
much less to say
about another high-
profile member of a
similar scheme. Who
just so happens to
be a Conservative
supporter...

decided to rule ou
r's smugness and me
ausing a conflagrat
ng act of self-immo

nting the possibili
and confess all, re
devote the rest of

"adviser" to JP Mo:
after he handed b

he stand at an inqu
he Hague, he took a
d Lansdowne Partner

absolutely

JIMMY CARR ROW
Cameron quiet on pop star tax claims

ssianic tendencies

g at his blatant h
d by the breathtak

tember 11 to the

ght years ago.

this egregious c

tax-dodgers

Spineless, self-serving, fatuous, knee-jerk reactionary, bandwagon-jumping, chancing opportunists. That just about sums up all our political parties this week.

If ever there was an argument for the old adage that whoever you vote for the government gets in, the current Tory and Labour rabble are it.

The obscene attempts at populism that have been spewing forth in recent days make Tony Blair's call for the release of Coronation Street con Deirdre Rachid sound like an Amnesty International campaign.

The irony of a prime minister responsible for the rendition and torture of his own citizens backing a campaign for the release of a fictional character was galling on a par with, well, what David Cameron did this week.

Yes, the bold PM waded into a row over comedian Jimmy Carr's tax affairs, condemning the performer for exploiting a tax-avoidance loophole while refusing to disclose his own financial arrangements.

Now, Carr is, as previously mentioned, a comic. Like him or not—and many don't—this column is guessing that what he is not is a financial lawyer in his spare time.

That the millionaire has been avoiding paying tax is of course disgraceful, but is it beyond the realms of possibility that, like most entertainers, he is clueless about money and pays an accountant to do all that?

An accountant—known as they are for their moral recti-
tude—who probably said this is a legal way of saving money?

In the grand scheme of things, it's not like what he did
was as cynical as what the Pope-in-waiting St Bono and his
chums in U2 did by shifting everything offshore, and I seem
to remember both Cameron and Blair. How fickle they are...

It's definitely not as dodgy as what Tory donor Lord Ashcroft
and Tory adviser Top Shop boss Sir Philip Green have done
and continue to do without a whimper of disapproval from
this morally upstanding government of multiple millionaires.
What could possibly be the connection there?

In fact a theme had begun to emerge as, when it emerged
on Thursday that the nation's new favourite monarch molester
Gary Barlow OBE and the rest of his facile boy band had a
remarkably similar arrangement to Carr, Cameron said naff
all. To add yet another layer of mendacity, Cameron faced
demands yesterday that the party pay back over £1 million
in cheap loans from firms which—wait for it—are registered
in tax havens in the British Virgin Islands, Liechtenstein and
elsewhere. Carr has apologised for his avoidance. Guess who
hasn't.

But it's not just the Tories—Labour have been going all-out
to show that when it comes to moral ambivalence they are
undoubtedly all in it together.

Which brings us to Ed Miliband ... who odiously, but predictably, played the immigration card yet again yesterday in
a speech which can adequately be summed up as "I'm not
racist, but..." It wasn't so much rivers of blood as rivers of
verbal diarrhoea.

As is customary in these matters, in the first five minutes he
name-checked his immigrant ancestors, saying how proud he
was of their courage.

You will no doubt recall that this was the exact same tactic employed by arch-Tory bigot Michael Howard just before he was going to stick the knife into asylum-seekers.

The ploy amusingly backfired on Howard as his relatives were from Transylvania and it just made him look even more like Nosferatu.

When Ann Widdecombe can slag you off for being weird and creepy, you know you've got problems.

Miliband's family also hail from eastern Europe and he boasted, for the umpteenth time, of his pride at his Jewish heritage.

And, if accidents of birth and religion are something to be proud of, fair enough. He then immediately went on to say how he would ensure that people just like his forebears would not be able to get in to the country.

Curiously, for one who is so keen on his family's heredity, he always he seems to have skipped the part where his father was a radical socialist. Funny that.

as right to kill up
"really honestly" believe

Diamond in

The Barclays chief exec had a terrible week, being forced to quit over the Libor rate-rigging scandal with only his £98m fortune and a multimillion-pound payoff to console him

decided to rule ou
r's smugness and me
ausing a conflagrat
of self-immo

DIAMOND SUNK BY LIBOR RATE SCAM

Millionaire Barclays banker quits as calls grow for a proper public probe

absolutely everyor

ssianic tendencies

g at his blatant h
d by the breathtak

tember 11 to the

ight years ago.

this egregious c

the rough

It's a strange, secretive cult, a quasi-religion with alien beliefs and an ideology based on a wilful distortion of history tailor-made to suit its own purposes.

Bankrolled and run by multimillionaires and politicians, its nefarious acolytes have infiltrated all walks of life.

Its public figurehead and arch-advocate is a lustrous-haired, perma-tanned, toothsome multimillionaire, the personification of the American dream. A high-level practitioner and messianic proselytiser.

A man, once the darling of the world's media, but whose increasingly erratic, some would say egregious, behaviour has led to an acrimonious and potentially costly divorce amid claims and counter-claims over disturbing practices within the organisation he most zealously represents.

Yes, it's not been a good week for Bob Diamond and Barclays, although it could have been a lot worse. Chelsea FC's second-richest supporter and Barclays chief exec Diamond was forced to resign from the firm he has helmed for just over a year—to spend more time with his money.

And what a lot of money it is. Diamond has an estimated personal fortune of £98 million, and that's before you add the £20m-plus payoff he has so nobly refused to waive.

Until recently this column had never heard of Libor and would probably have assumed it was a kind of eastern European lager. And to be honest, like the Higgs boson particle, it still does not really understand it except that it's probably quite important.

Also like the "god particle," it would appear that most of those investigating it don't really get it either—at least that's what it looked like in Parliament the other day.

There was a strange feeling of deja vu when Diamond appeared before the select committee this week, what with a massively wealthy chief exec being given a less than intensive grilling by a gaggle of showboating politicians. Now where have we seen that before...

They say sorry is the hardest word, which might be why both the dastardly dingo Rupert Murdoch and Bob "bank job" Diamond didn't really bother.

Oh, they made some of the right noises, they both expressed their "shock" and abhorrence at getting caught—er, I mean the appalling behaviour that had occurred on their watch. Then in the next breath they basically said: "Nothing to do with me, squire."

The committees in question also went through the motions and appeared to put on a good show, but with one or two honourable exceptions you could tell their hearts weren't really in it and in actuality both Diamond and Murdoch were probably amazed just what an easy ride they got.

In each case the committee's line of questioning was as toothless as a geriatric sheep with gingivitis, more interested in point-scoring and pontificating than actually getting any real answers.

There is of course an obvious reason for this. In both the News Corp and banking scandals all three parties are steeped up to their necks in it.

It seems like every week there is a feigned show of contrition and manufactured outrage from these pampered politicos in the coalition and the Blairites in the shadow cabinet—sometimes more than once.

You'd think they'd be better at it by now, but no. They're like the toddler who, when you ask why the wallpaper suddenly has a permanent marker motif, blames the cat. When you point out you don't have a cat and they've got the pen in their hand they throw a tantrum and say they'll phone Childline.

Which is more or less exactly what both Ed Balls and George Osborne did on Thursday. Two allegedly "respected" economists supposed to be debating one of the worst financial scandals for, ooh, at least a month.

Instead we were treated to a blustering bawl-fest of chest-puffing and self-righteous outrage. Balls assumed his usual role of bellowing, mad-eyed bison and Osborne ducked behind the dispatch box and reappeared in the now familiar sneering guise of Flashman.

To give you a flavour of the "debate" it went along the lines of "How dare you?" "Nooo, how dare you?" How dare either of them.

as right to kill up 1
"really honestly" believe

Oodles of

Outrage in the
tabloids as Games
flame-bearers
were found
selling their
souvenir
torches on
eBay, when
avarice has
no part
to play
in the Olympics.
Apart from Coke.
And McDonald's.
And Atos. And Dow
'Bhopal Disaster'
Chemical. And...

decided to rule ou
r's smugness and me
ausing a conflagrat
ng act of self-immo

THE OLYMPIC TAINT

2012 London Games' links to toxic corporations
threaten to ruin its legacy, campaigners warn

he stand at an inqu
he Hague, he took a
d Lansdowne Partner

absolutely everyor

LONDON 2012: OLYMPIC TORCH RELAY
Flame goes out as bearers rush to sell on eBay

g at his blatant h
d by the breathtak

tember 11 to the 1

ight years ago.

this egregious c

Olympic gold

A pparently there's some sort of jamboree or something going on this weekend but this column is determined—like Nelson clasping a spyglass to his blind eye—to remain stubbornly ignorant of the matter.

And besides there are more important matters to discuss. Namely the continuing dual farces of the Olympics and the coalition, both of which seem intent on plunging themselves deeper into the mire of mediocrity and murky media manipulation.

In recent days certain sections of the fourth estate have worked themselves into a state of frothing apoplexy over the fact that a number of those relaying the Olympic flame across this septic isle have been selling them for cold hard cash on eBay. Making people pay over two hundred quid for the privilege of keeping their tacky souvenir of the Games is fine apparently, but when the plebs start getting in on the act that's a no-no.

It has been claimed that those attempting to make a few bob from auctioning off their baubles—many of them for charitable causes—are not in line with the Olympian spirit.

That may be the case but it's certainly in keeping with the ethos of this Olympics, which is basically sell everything you can and if it doesn't move quickly enough slap a brand on it.

Yes, apparently grasping monetarism and avarice is the sole preserve of the Olympic organising committee.

Likewise getting Dow Chemical, Coke, McDonald's, Atos and God knows who else to sponsor a sporting event is perfectly acceptable, we're told.

An estimated 10-30,000 Indians and counting have died in Bhopal with hundreds of thousands permanently injured as a result of the toxic leak at the Union Carbide plant and Dow, which now owns the firm, is still resisting payments to the victims. It appears to be perfectly happy to bung a shedload of money at Locog though.

Handing the advertising rights to Dow for a dodgy backhander is possibly the crassest thing this government has done yet. Apart from the small matter of giving the firm responsible for booting thousands of people off disability benefits the key sponsorship role for the Paralympics, that is … that's like getting Vlad the Impaler to sponsor a kebab shop.

Personally I'm surprised BAE Systems haven't tried to get in on the act. After all they're entitled, having done more to make countless people in developing countries disabled than most.

McDonald's and Coca-Cola, along with Heineken, have been granted exclusive rights to the food and drink franchises at the Games and a small bottle of beer will cost punters four and a half quid. That's one way to stop binge drinking I suppose.

Readers may recall that the firm producing the official Olympic and Paralympic mascots got into a spot of bother recently when it emerged they were produced in sweatshop conditions.

Well, you need kids to make them don't you? It takes tiny hands to do all those fiddly stitches. It's probably one of the recommendations in the Beecroft report.

Meanwhile, so zealously guarded is the Olympic cash cow, er, I mean iconic symbolism that they ruthlessly crack down on any unauthorised usage by criminal pirates.

In this case that would be 81-year-old granny Joy Tomkins who was threatened with prosecution for breach of copyright after she put a second-hand doll in a home-made knitted T-shirt and shorts emblazoned with "GB 2012" and the Olympic rings into her local church bring-and-buy sale.

Fortunately trading standards swooped to avert the disaster, but like a 100m medallist passing a drug test it was a close-run thing.

One person who has been a vocal advocate for the Games— and the Murdoch empire—is cockney rhyming slang's favourite son, Culture Secretary Jeremy Hunt. I'm reliably informed he's definitely for the high jump.

Mini-Murdoch

The phone-hacking scandal seemed to have claimed its biggest scalp yet when James Murdoch stepped down as News International chief. But on closer inspection it wasn't so much resignation as relocation for Rupert's heir apparent

JAMES MURDOCH QUITS AS NEWS INTERNATIONAL CHAIRMAN

as right to kill up
"really honestly" believed

decided to rule out
r's smugness and me
ausing a conflagrat
ng act of self-immo

he Hague, he took a
d Lansdowne Partner

absolutely everyor

ssianic tendencies

g at his blatant h
d by the breathtak

tember 11 to the]

ight years ago.

probably really ho̵̵̵̵̵̵̵ly believed he was right to ...sn't ... they
...l mass...

goes west

rigger some form of chain reaction cau......agratio
...t and therefore an unwitting act of self-immola

When is a resignation not a mea culpa? When it's a scion of the Murdoch empire apparently. This week mini-Murdoch not so much threw himself on his sword as gave himself a minor paper cut with it as the fallout from the hacking scandal continued to pile sack after sack of ordure at his Wapping front door.

At first glance the gullible—and Sky News for some reason this column can't quite put its finger on—appeared to see this as some vestigial modicum of shame or, at the very least, a sacrificial head tumbling into the wicker basket of public opinion.

But if anyone was naive enough to believe that they were soon disabused of the notion.

In a statement accompanying the announcement the company said James Murdoch was stepping down from his role as head of News International "following his relocation to the company's headquarters in New York."

"We are all grateful for James's leadership at News International and across Europe and Asia, where he has made lasting contributions to the group's strategy in paid digital content and its efforts to improve and enhance governance programmes," said the paterfamilias of the ongoing pantomime that is the Murdoch empire, Rupert.

"He has demonstrated leadership," he added, apparently straight-faced. And then came what is known in certain circles as the clincher.

"Now that he has moved to New York, James will continue to assume a variety of essential corporate leadership mandates with particular focus on important pay-TV businesses and broader international operations."

So, not a "resignation" as much as a "relocation." Some might even call it a promotion.

Murdoch fils, showing he lacks none of his father's brass neck, claimed that he deeply appreciated the "dedication of my many talented colleagues at News International who work tirelessly to inform the public."

These would be the colleagues he sacked at the News of the Screws to save his and Rebekah Brooks's necks presumably.

As for the public he professes to serve, wouldn't they be the ones who were hacked without their knowledge by scumbag hacks at the NoW and the Sun?

This week has seen a senior Met officer accuse News International in a court of law of operating a network of corruption including bent cops, cadging civil servants and at least one shifty squaddie. Let's face it, none of that is exactly surprising and anyone with even a passing knowledge of Fleet Street's more clandestine practices wouldn't have batted an eyelid except that it was a member of the Met that said it.

One wonders if Deputy Assistant Commissioner Sue Akers would have been quite so forthright if the newly launched Sun hadn't spent the last few weeks putting the boot into her.

It's quite a turnaround for News International, attacking a cop who's investigating you—they normally bought them dinner.

Then we had possibly the standout revelation of the week— that the Met had given Brooks a horse. A bloody horse! Maybe it was the cops' equivalent of a loyalty card bonus—you get your collar felt so many times and you get a free pony.

Given Brooks's involvement with the Don Corleone of the media world it's amazing it came back in one piece. There are any number of pillows its head could've ended up on. Ross Kemp's for a start.

But perhaps the most intriguing aspect of this week is the apparent rejuvenation of Rupert himself.

During his performance before the Commons select committee scant months ago he made himself look like Tutankhamun's granddad. Curious then that this month he's like a dingo in an outback branch of Mothercare.

hearing I had reluctantly decided to rule
sheer enormity of Blair's smugness and me
form of chain reaction causing a conflagrati
and therefore an unwitting act of self-immo

did was try to link September 11 to the Ir
cular claim didn't hold water eight years a
evidence to support this egregious claim be

were carried out mainly by

urprise, surprise. Tony Blair thinks he wa
illion people in an illegal war because he
e was right.

ell, that was worth £250k of public money
nows how much in inquiry salaries, wasn't

arles Manson probably really honestly bel:
every egomani   derer in

Spooks & Coppers

Blair was always going to allow his messi:
k—yet again.

I'm a model

The Metropolitan Police cast their net wider than ever--and alarmed the Advertising Standards Authority as well as students across Britain-- with an ad asking us to report anyone who doesn't have a bank card and likes to keep their curtains closed. Meanwhile, the PM recruited credit ratings agencies to spy on benefit claimants

CAMERON LAUNCHES FRESH WAR ON POOR

Campaigners warn benefit 'bounty hunter' plan will bring more poverty

s right to kill up
"really honestly" believeu

decided to rule ou
r's smugness and men
ausing a conflagrat
ng act of self-immo

nting the possibili
and confess all, re
devote the rest of

"adviser" to JP Mo
s after he handed b

olutely everyor

ssianic tendencies

g at his blatant h
d by the breathtak

tember 11 to the

ght years ago.

this egregious c

terrorist

I am reeling from the revelation this week that I am the Met's definition of a terror suspect.

According to Slipper of the Yard and his chums in the flying squad, the definition of a terrorist suspect is someone who doesn't like using a credit card, doesn't know many of their neighbours and sometimes keeps their curtains closed during the day.

Guilty, guilty and thrice guilty.

Not only do I not have a credit card, I won't even use those automated check-out things. Well, stick me in a cave and call me Osama.

In fact, not only am I apparently a terrorist by the Met's definition, almost everyone I know is one! And most of them don't even have beards or an Irish accent.

It's enough to make you paranoid. Maybe while I sleep I am secretly working towards jihad, or the armed struggle for a 32-county Ireland. I wondered why I kept waking up furiously tugging at the cord for the roller blinds shouting "Detonate! Detonate!" Suddenly everything is clear.

It's clear that the Met are a bunch of testosterone-crazed idiots.

Thankfully the Advertising Standards Agency had a modicum of good sense and told them to wise up in no uncertain terms. Can you imagine the mayhem that would have caused? What's next? Wearing dark glasses a sign you're a paedophile?

Smoking a cigarette a sign you're a serial arsonist? A penchant for cross-dressing means you're a High Court judge?

Well, actually, the last one is quite a good indicator, but you get the point.

It's not as if we don't have enough lazy, bigoted stereotyping to contend with in this country, with the abundance of casual racism, homophobia and Tory voters. Now we are being encouraged to persecute and inform on shy people with bad credit who like to watch Countdown.

In fact when you think about it, by its unique brand of logic, the Met's new key targets are pensioners and dope-smoking students.

I know bin Laden isn't exactly a spring chicken, but I'm fairly sure he doesn't go on Saga holidays and I don't think he's permanently got the munchies. They'd have caught him ages ago outside a 24-hour garage with a basket full of Kit Kats and Monster Munch.

This is not the first time the Met's PR department has made a balls-up of erstwhile England keeper Robert Green-style proportions. A few years ago, it offered a bounty for officers who signed up black or ethnic minority recruits to help foster diversity in the force.

Given the Met's usual way of dealing with people of an ethnic minority persuasion, this probably led to quite a few cops abducting people from the street and bringing them in bound and gagged in the boot of their panda. This is a force, remember, which believes that being Brazilian in possession of an Oyster card is a capital offence.

Speaking of bounties, David Cameron has decided to get in on the act this week, announcing that he will employ credit ratings firms to snoop on benefit claimants on a no dirt, no fee basis. Well, that's a stroke of genius, isn't it? Axe almost half of the DWP's staff then employ outside touts to do your dirty work for you.

If we're going to go down that road, why not make it really interesting. Let's employ real bounty hunters, like in the movies, to hunt down, taser and drag back Lord Ashcroft and the rest of these tax-dodging non-dom Tory donors.

We could televise it and place bets how long it will take to catch a Tory peer in a net—they squirm a lot, so it's not as easy as it looks. People on benefits could watch it during the daytime, with the curtains closed.

is right to kill up 1
"really honestly" believe

The bent

decided to rule out
r's smugness and men
ausing a conflagrat:
ng act of self-immo

31 years after the
fact an official
report finally
admitted the police
killed anti-fascist
protester Blair
Peach--
and it was
made clear
that no-
one would
ever face
justice.
Which came
as no
surprise
to the
families of
Harry Stanley, Jean
Charles de Menezes
or Ian Tomlinson

nting the possibili
and confess all, re
devote the rest of

Bring lying police officers to justice

Internal report into Blair Peach's death points finger at riot squad

ssianic tendencies

g at his blatant h
d by the breathtak

ptember 11 to the 1

ight years ago.

this egregious c

blue line

W ell, some things never change do they? Yet again this week we were graphically reminded of the fact that when it comes to "great British justice" there is no such thing, especially if you're up against a bunch of bent coppers.

Tuesday finally saw the release of the much-anticipated Cass report into the murder of New Zealand teacher and anti-fascist Blair Peach by the thick blue line of the Met's Special Patrol Group (SPG).

The report came out almost exactly 31 years to the day after Peach was killed by a riot cop—or cops—following an anti-National Front demonstration in Southall on April 23 1979. The publication was welcomed by Peach's partner Celia Stubbs and confirmed what many had long believed.

The Met response also confirmed what many of us suspected, namely that no-one is ever going to be brought to justice for the heinous crime.

This is hardly surprising. When you look at the litany of police brutality cases over the years, many of which involve London's finest, convictions are about as frequent as appearances by Halley's comet.

The infamy of the SPG is well founded. Like that other group of paramilitary thugs the Black and Tans, the Met's shock troops revelled in their brutal image. A raid on their locker room following Peach's murder discovered knives, crowbars and coshes.

There is apparently a ban on police officers being members of extremist organisations—although I would argue that the SPG was pretty much an extremist organisation—but, if this raid was anything to go by, having your own personal shrine to the Third Reich is OK. "Well, it brightens the place up a bit dunnit?"

Cass himself recommended prosecution of three SPG members for perverting the course of justice. Cops covering up for each other? What an outrageous concept. Next you'll be telling me that suspects aren't just really careless when it comes to going down stairs.

But perhaps the most chilling aspect of the Cass report was a single paragraph which tells you more about the police mentality than anything else in the report.

Cass said that the demonstration was "an extremely violent volatile and ugly situation where there was serious disturbance by what can be classed as a 'rebellious crowd'."

He then states: "Without condoning the death I refer to Archbold 38th edition para 2528: 'In case of riot or rebellious assembly the officers endeavouring to disperse the riot are justified in killing them at common law if the riot cannot otherwise be suppressed'." So this is a, now former, senior Met commander saying quite bluntly that the law is entitled to kill demonstrators. Well, that fills you with confidence regarding our criminal justice system, doesn't it?

Met Chief Paul Stephenson said the report made "uncomfortable reading." Something of an understatement I'd imagine. He also attempted to suggest that this showed how far things had come since 1979. Oh, really? Tell that to the family of Harry Stanley, who was gunned down for the heinous crime of carrying a table leg and being in possession of a Scottish accent.

Or the family of Jean Charles de Menezes. He was guilty of being Brazilian in a public place. Tell that to the family of Ian Tomlinson, who one year on from his death following an assault by an officer of the Territorial Support Group—the rebranded SPG—are still waiting to see if any prosecution will be brought.

They say justice is blind, but when it comes to the Met it would appear it's also deaf and dumb.

is right to kill up 1
"really honestly" believe

Olympic ring

Just when the
London security
lockdown seemed
like it couldn't
get any more OTT
ministers outdid
themselves with a
hare-brained scheme
to station surface-
to-air missile
batteries atop
blocks of flats in
densely populated
areas

decided to rule ou1
r's smugness and me1
ausing a conflagrat.
ng act of self-immo

nting the possibili
and confess all, re
devote the rest of

"adviser" to JP Mo1
s after he handed b

he stand at an inqu
he Hague, he took a
d Lansdowne Partner

OLYMPIC WEAPONS

Residents launch legal bid to block roof missile plans

ately everyo1

g at his blatant h
d by the breathtak

tember 11 to the 1

ight years ago.

this egregious c

# of steel

Estate agent: "Yes, it's a compact and bijou west-facing property in a delightful block of converted mill buildings in east London with plenty of light. Close to all the amenities and with the added bonus of a state-of-the art security system."

Customer: "Oh really? Well, that's good because we have been burgled before haven't we, darling?"

"Believe me, madam, that will not be a problem with this luxury property."

"Oh yes, we noted that it was a gated community. What other security is there? Security guard patrols? Motion detectors?"

"(under breath) A battalion of armed soldiers."

"I suppose it's fully alarmed?"

"Oh, yes. All the tenants are highly alarmed, some might even say terrified...

"Pardon?"

"Nothing, nothing ... have I shown you the spacious kitchen with ceramic hob?"

To each other: "And I suppose with the Olympic redevelopment it will increase its value after all."

"If it stays up."

"Excuse me?"

"Er, I said with a bit of luck."

"And what are the tenants upstairs like?"

"Oh, quiet, quiet, mostly, very ... disciplined. You'll hardly know they're there, what with the camouflage."

"We did worry slightly as it's quite close to the airport's flight path isn't it?"

"Not for long."

Yes, in keeping with the true spirit of the Olympics, the government, not content with turning half of Hackney into a ring of steel and planning to taser anyone consuming the wrong brand of sandwich or beverage, has decided in its infinite wisdom to press ahead with its plans to force residents to have a full-on surface-to-air missile system on their roofs.

What kind of brain-dead psychopaths install Rapier missile systems on blocks of flats? Well, the MoD obviously.

For a start, if the recoil from launching a battery of missiles at an alleged airborne terrorist threat doesn't demolish the entire building, where is the plane going to come down? On central London, that's where.

There is of course a precedent for acts of terrorism at the Olympics, but al-Qaida would have to try bloody hard to bring more chaos to the capital than Transport for London and Boris Johnson do on a daily basis. And they get paid for it.

In fact, any self-respecting terrorist would probably take one look at the place and assume someone had beaten them to it.

But on to other, less London-centric but equally bizarre news.

This week evidence has emerged that the former Tory MP for Totnes, now deceased, was a spy for the Czech secret service throughout the '60s.

The late Ray Mawby, described as a "Conservative with a strong trade union background," was nevertheless on the right of the party and opposed the legalisation of homosexuality, so he was definitely in the right camp.

He was also a bit of a boozer and gambler by all accounts, which may suggest the reason for his covert activities for which he was apparently paid £100 a time, according to a signed receipt found in the Czech archives.

It's not like a Tory to sign a receipt—it's normally cash in a brown paper bag.

Many have expressed shock at the allegation that a Tory should spy for the communists, but that is based on the false assumption that the Tories have any form of ideology or moral code.

And anyway they've taken money from just about everyone else both individually and collectively, so why not the Czechs?

Mawby is thought to be the first Tory to have been unmasked as a covert agent for hire in such a manner, although Ken Clarke does have a similar arrangement with Oddbins.

The documents would seem to suggest however that, when it came to being an intelligence source, Mawby may have been a bit of a dunce and was more likely to give you the winner of the 2.30 at Aintree than be able to divulge sensitive state secrets.

The meetings with his handler must have been hilarious.

"Have you seen the Grey Squirrel?"

"Yes, thousands of the buggers. Vermin I call them! But I'll bet you a fiver that one gets up the tree first. Drinky-poo?"

s right to kill up 1
"really honestly" believed

Whitewash

After weeks of
scandal the
government finally
released details
of MPs'
expenses
claims--
but covered
in more
black marker
than a Rolf
Harris sketchbook.
And claims that the
new Iraq inquiry
would be held in
public rang hollow
with veterans of
security cover-ups
  like Bloody Sunday

decided to rule ou
r's smugness and mer
ausing a conflagrat
ng act of self-immo

nting the possibili

EXPENSES SCANDAL

**Blackout
on MPs' claims**

FULL AND FRANK:
This ampersand for the
Conservative MP
Andrew Mackay
(below)

Campaigners aghast as parliamentary expenses list omits swathes of key details

e stand at an inqu
e Hague, he took a
d Lansdowne Partner

absolutely everyor

ssianic tendencies

CHILCOT INQUIRY
**'Partial' Iraq war
hearings slammed**
Stop the War condemns failure to consult bereaved families

g at his blatant h
d by the breathtak

tember 11 to the 1

ight years ago.

this egregious c

lay
cha
r s
rtm

fel
hir
. be

is l
ici

eek
  th
pop
ks

bab
lf.

was

on

thi

icul

probably really ho...ly believed he was right to ...hey

and blackout

...gger some form of chain reaction cau... ...gratio
...therefore an unwitting act of self-immola

So the government, flying in the face of all logic, hung onto its expenses report for weeks and weeks despite the fact that the majority of the sleaze had already been plastered across the front of the Torygraph.

And then when they do release the document, it's got more blackouts than London during the blitz.

Still, at least we know why it took them so long now—repetitive strain injury from all that colouring in. The sheer idiocy of this beggars belief.

If the government had had an ounce of wit about them, they would have put the whole lot on the internet as soon as the whole sordid business came to light and let the greedy buggers fend for themselves. At least it would have stopped the interminable dribble of mildly titillating but basically identical stories day after day after day.

But there was some bizarre news this week. Yes, we may have got a file of expenses claims with more holes in it than a Jeffrey Archer alibi, but it now seems that the government might actually hold some of the Iraq inquiry in public.

Not that it matters of course. Governments only ever announce inquiries when they're damn sure what the result is going to be.

We don't have to look back far to recall the Wodehousian farce that was the Butler inquiry, where the immaculately groomed and highly droll manservant was called upon to spare the blushes of his hapless and fatuous master who'd got himself into a bit of a scrape over a dodgy dossier and some non-existent WMDs. What a lark! And all wrapped up in time for tiffin.

And then we had the whitewash extraordinaire of the Hutton debacle.

Tired of persistent smears on your otherwise unblemished reputation? Stubborn stains on your character getting you down? Try new improved Huttomatic! Simply drop a pinch of Huttomatic in with your dirty laundry, place on full spin for a couple of weeks and hey presto! Your tawdry briefs emerge whiter than white. Small print: May bring some people out in a rash, no money back, no guarantee.

But that's this? Even those two celebrated purveyors of truth and justice the Tony Blair way have come forward and said the new inquiry should be held in public.

Well bits of it anyway, you know, the bits where Labour doesn't look too bad if you squint and close one eye and knock back half a bottle of sherry.

The bits Gordon Brown says it's all right for us to see. I covered the Bloody Sunday inquiry for three years so I know a little bit about state censorship.

Secret witnesses in the cabinet of mendacity (as one legal friend of mine referred to the witness box at Derry's Guildhall).

Brave squaddies cowering behind anonymity and personal immunity clauses, lying through their teeth about murdering unarmed civilians over 30 years ago and then callously branding them paramilitaries and nailbombers.

No-one admitting what the agenda was on January 30 1972 and definitely nobody taking responsibility. It's all horribly familiar.

One thing is for sure though. If they went that far in censoring the MPs' expenses there'll be more frenzied use of a marker pen than at a Rolf Harris convention before we finally get to see the Iraq report.

Brainless

Fresh from revelations that MI5 couldn't even track down suspected communist Charlie Chaplin's south London birthplace, we learned of a rare triumph for our spooks, who concluded that Hitler had a 'messiah complex' and didn't trust the Jews. And it only took them till 1942 to work it out

HOME NEWS

NATIONAL ARCHIVES

Chaplin 'born and bred in south London'

by Tony Patey

ALL MI5 had to do was send a spook out from its headquarters and across Lambeth Bridge and the mystery of Charlie Chaplin's birthplace would have been cleared up.

It has always been thought that the star of The Great Dictator and The Gold Rush was born in Walworth, south London, on April 16 1889.

When the FBI — on the hunt for communists — asked MI5 for information about the actor's background the nation's finest couldn't find any record of his birth at Somerset House.

So, according to a partly released file by the National Archives, a report concluded: "It would seem that Chaplin was either not born in this country or that his birth was under some other

the King family in the Elephant and Castle they would have got them the facts. They certainly knew his folks.

Father of three John King told the Morning Star yesterday that his paternal grandmother Mabel King knew the Chaplin family, but she was certainly not one of his fans.

Mr King, acting assistant manager at a local print office, died in 1972, actually went to school with Charlie's brother Sydney — they went to St Mary's School.

His mother Ethel told the Star: "My mother Alice Stowe, died in 1972, actually went

Great-grandmother Mabel, 82, said her

[partially visible fragments in margins: "right to kill up", "really honestly" believed, "decided to rule out", "r's smugness and men", "ausing a conflagrat", "ng act of self-immo", "nting the possibili", "and confess all, re", "devote the rest of", "to JP Mor", "anded ba", "an inqu", "e took a", "Partner", "everyor", "ndencies", "olatant h", "by the breathtak", "tember 11 to the", "ght years ago.", "this egregious c"]

intelligence

You really have to wonder at the calibre of Britain's spies and "intelligence" community. Not their penchant for torture, lies and secret evidence which have been well documented in recent years, but their sheer historical propensity for idiocy.

A few months ago it was revealed that when the FBI, in the grip of J Edgar Hoover's anti-communist paranoia, asked MI5 to investigate Charlie Chaplin's background they couldn't even find out that he was born in south London.

This week "secret" documents have come to light providing an even more eye-opening insight into the world of second world war intelligence and espionage.

A psychological analysis of another legendary dodgy tache-sporter, compiled by a Cambridge academic in 1942, gave the following earth-shattering revelations. Hitler had a bit of a "messiah complex" and was paranoid about the Jews. Suddenly it all becomes clear! If only we'd known.

Now, some might have thought that the fact that he'd established a "Thousand Year Reich" and that he'd already invaded half of Europe might have been a hint as to the former.

You don't get many self-effacing dictators—like old Etonians, being an egomaniac kind of goes with the job description.

The rabid speeches, self-aggrandising rallies and the foaming at the mouth could possibly have been clues as well.

And, oh I dunno, three-and-a-half years beforehand in 1938 a certain event known as Kristallnacht might have given at least an indication of the latter. This could be a whole new thing—retrospective prognostication.

To make it all the more surreal, when this story broke on the wires it was strictly embargoed.

It's 70 bloody years old and Hitler's been dead since 1945. I don't think we're exactly in danger of breaching national security here.

The document was apparently found among a collection of papers belonging to the family of Mark Abrams, a social scientist who worked with the BBC's overseas propaganda analysis unit and the psychological warfare board during the war.

Scott Anthony, who stumbled upon the report, said: "I could not believe it when we found this document. I was completely shocked and I just kept reading it over and over again—it really is a fascinating piece of history."

I know the BBC has something of a reputation for being late in breaking a story, but this is ridiculous.

Written by Joseph McCurdy, the aforementioned Oxbridge academic, it refers to earlier signs of "morbid tendencies," classifying these as "shamanism," "epilepsy" and "paranoia."

I think planning extermination camps and the mass murder of homosexuals, Gypsies, Jews and communists could probably be described as "morbid." Bit harsh on epileptics though.

Intriguingly the bit the Telegraph chose to highlight was that "Hitler thought he could divine the weather." Well, so did Michael Fish but that doesn't make him a fascist.

But then the Tory Party's official propaganda organ might not want to dwell on a psychological profile focusing on God complexes, paranoia and the persecution of minorities given the party's traditional leadership and policies.

The fact that it's taken 70 years for this to come to light makes one wonder what stunning revelations we have to look forward to in the years to come. An incendiary document from 1986 saying that Margaret Thatcher may have issues when it comes to the miners and Argentina?

Coincidentally—or was it?—this week also saw the US publish a cache of documents retrieved from the Pakistani compound of Osama bin Laden. If anything this was even less interesting although there were a few intriguing oddities.

The most surreal was that he was apparently planning to encourage Irish Catholics, disillusioned with the church over the never-ending child abuse scandals, to convert to Islam. He'd obviously never been to a Feis.

If he knew anything about Ireland he would have approached the Free Presbyterians—half of Ian Paisley's mob seem to think they're in the Taliban anyway.

The other bizarre item was the fact that the man who had spent decades carving a name out for himself as the world's most infamous terrorist was apparently considering rebranding al-Qaida.

What as? Just Jihad? I Can't Believe It's Not Bin Laden?

as right to kill up 1
"really honestly" believe

It's Plod's

The Met's new top cop found the job busier than he bargained for as he was forced to tackle a series of scandals involving undercover officers misbehaving-- including one accused of testifying under a false name and another who slept with the activists he was supposed to be spying on

decided to rule ou?
r's smugness and mer
ausing a conflagrat.
ng act of self-immo

nting the possibili
s all, re

LONDON FORCE ACCUSED OF 'DISASTROUS MISTAKES'
Met faces flak over false trial evidence
Undercover officer accused of giving false name under oath

he stand at an inqu
ne Hague, he took a
d Lansdowne Partner

absolutely everyor

ssianic tendencies

g at his blatant h
d by the breathtak

INFILTRATION
Greenpeace: Police officer 'was a spy'

tember 11 to the 1

ight years ago.

this egregious c

honest truth

You almost have to feel sorry for new top cop, the extravagantly monickered Bernard Hogan-Howe. One minute you're in a cushy job at the Inspectorate of Constabulary, the rigorous internal vetting body whose primary role appears to consist of regurgitating the now legendary phrase "Move along, move along, nothing to see here." The next you're in charge of the Keystone Kops.

Hogan-Howe sounds like he should be at the head of the Berkshire hunt blowing a bugle and yelling tally-ho but has more the appearance of someone desperately herding cats with a water cannon.

The Met, never one to hide its flashing blue light under a bushel when it comes to boasting about its "successes" in the fight against global terrorism and banging up wrong 'uns, has been strangely reluctant to stick its pointy-hatted head above the parapet in recent months.

What with all the backhanders from hacks, cosy meetings between investigating officers and News International executives, the forced resignation of Sir Paul Stephenson after it was revealed he'd taken a freebie holiday at a health spa … well, you would be hard-pressed to throw an extendable baton over your shoulder and not hit someone up to their necks in nefarious doings.

And that's not to mention the allegations of copulating undercover cops, agents provocateurs and dubious convictions which resurfaced yet again this week with all the welcome timing of dysentery at a wedding.

First there was the outing of Bob Lambert, an academic highly regarded in some circles and former head of Special Branch's "Muslim contact unit" as the Met's equivalent of George Smiley. Lambert was revealed to have infiltrated Greenpeace for a number of years in the 1980s as well as having run Special Branch's spook squad which spied on anti-fascists and other organisations in spectacularly mendacious fashion.

On Wednesday, Hogan-Howe had been preparing to publish his soft-soap report into the debacle surrounding the actions of undercover officer Mark Kennedy, which saw the trial of environmental activists collapse after evidence he had gathered which would have proved their innocence was suppressed.

Intriguingly the evidence was recorded on his specially modified Casio watch in fine cinematic spook tradition.

Ironically it is possession of a Casio watch which has seen many people banged up in Guantanamo Bay as alleged al-Qaida bomb-makers, according to briefing documents for interrogators.

It would appear the firm has unwittingly cornered the market in espionage and international terrorism, although you probably won't see it on an advertising slogan any time soon.

But to return to Hogan-Howe, mere hours before he was due to present his report at a much-fanfared press conference in London, it all exploded in his face with yet another hugely embarrassing disclosure.

This time it was the allegation that another police spy, Jim Boyling, had given evidence under a false name during the trial of Reclaim the Streets protesters he had been infiltrating to protect his cover.

All rather unfortunate really, especially when you were about to publish the findings of an investigation widely expected to exonerate the force as a whole of any wrongdoing.

It's hardly unknown for cops to be "imaginative" in terms of giving their evidence on the stand but at least the court normally has a fair idea of who they are. How does that work?

Clerk of the court: "Do you solemnly swear to tell the truth, the whole truth and nothing but the truth so help you God?"

"Well, when you say truth…"

But then, when we've got a government so crooked it'd need help screwing its trousers on, and which is demanding secret trials for torture cases to cover up its own guilt, what can you expect?

Ken Clarke said this week it was becoming "fashionable" for people to challenge the evidence of the security services in court. I wonder why?

hearing I had reluctantly decided to rule

sheer enormity of Blair's smugness and me

form of chain reaction causing a conflagrati

and therefore an unwitting act of self-immo

did was try to link September 11 to the Ir

cular claim didn't hold water eight years a

evidence to support this egregious claim be

were carried out mainly by

urprise, surprise. Tony Blair thinks he wa
illion people in an illegal war because he
e was right.

ell, that was worth £250k of public money
nows how much in inquiry salaries, wasn't

harles Manson probably really honestly bel:
every egomani derer in

US Presidents &
Other Extremists

Blair was always going to allow his messi
—yet again.

as right to kill up
"really honestly" believe

Beyond

With the US reeling
from the death of
six people in an
assassination
attempt on
Congresswoman
Gabrielle
Giffords, it
was a bad idea
for Sarah Palin
to mouth off
at critics of
her campaign
targeting
leading
Democrats--
including
Giffords--with
rifle crosshairs.
But Palin never
met a bad idea she
didn't embrace

decided to rule ou
r's smugness and me
ausing a conflagrat.
f self-immo

ARIZONA SHOOTING

US in shock over fatal shooting

Questions raised over impact of
Tea Party 'target' campaigns

absolutely everyor

ssianic tendencies

g at his blatant h
d by the breathtak

tember 11 to the

ight years ago.

this egregious c

the Palin

The sickening behaviour of Sarah Palin and her Tea Party numpties reached new levels of cowardice and mendacity this week when they attempted to distance themselves from the multiple murders in Arizona.

It is true that there is no definite evidence that the gunman who so callously opened fire in a supermarket car park killing six people and critically injuring a Democrat senator is a member of this odious organisation—or even a sympathiser.

But if—as was the case with Palin—you have, oh, I don't know ... a map posted on your website targeting, quite literally, the politician in question and a number of others who had supported Barack Obama's less than radical health-care reforms, framed in rifle crosshairs ... if also you were a tub-thumping evangelist for lax gun control, had engaged in smearing, denigrating your opponents and exploiting rhetoric which makes the late and unlamented NRA mascot Charlton Heston sound like one of the flower power generation...

If then for example that particular politician, Congresswoman Gabrielle Giffords, ended up being gunned down, along with a nine-year-old child, you would think that at the very least you might pause to reflect on your actions...

Anyone who naively assumed that even intellectually stunted bottom feeders like Palin and her cronies might actually feel any genuine sorrow for the victims of the massacre were firmly disabused of that notion later in the week.

In a recorded statement Palin took to the airwaves several days after the event to round on the media and her political opponents for picking on her.

Earlier in the week one of her fellow Tea Party loons Mark Meckler told a website: "To see the left exploit this for political advantage—some people have no conscience. It's genuinely revolting … I think it sinks to the level of evil."

Let's just take a moment to absorb the full extent of the staggering hypocrisy of that statement.

It's akin to Nick Griffin when, following his Custer moment at the Barking and Dagenham polls, he said he'd lost because foreign people hadn't voted for him.

But I digress. Calamity Palin apparently bridled at the fact that people had pointed out that her egregious behaviour probably hadn't helped the situation.

Curiously, her public announcement happened to coincide roughly with the time that Barack Obama was actually in Arizona offering support to the community, not that any connection should be made there of course.

Now Palin has done many, many crass and offensive things in her brief spell in the electoral limelight but even by her standards this was grotesque.

The gun-toting reactionary throwback could only be bothered to grudgingly reference the families of those slaughtered before moving on to her real purpose, attempting to cover her arse.

To pick just a few choice comments, she spoke of the "vigorous and spirited public debates during elections"—that would be her hate-filled haranguing of her opponents then.

She claimed that "there are those who claim political rhetoric is to blame for the despicable act of this deranged, apparently apolitical criminal."

And she went on: "We must reject the idea that every time a law's broken, society is guilty rather than the lawbreaker."

Then, my personal favourite, she condemned those who "mock" the US's greatness, "by being intolerant of differing opinion and seeking to muzzle dissent with shrill cries of imagined insults."

Sounds like every Tea Party rally since they crawled out from under their respective rocks.

Now I'm not saying Sarah Palin is directly responsible for what happened in Arizona, I'm just saying that her contribution to US society is on a par with that of herpes.

as right to kill up 1
"really honestly" believed

Yes, we can.

The first
anniversary of
Obama's
inauguration
was a good
time to take
stock of his
achievements.
Which, with
Guantanamo
still open,
health-care
reform stalled
and war high on his
agenda despite a
Nobel peace prize,
didn't add up to
all that much

decided to rule out
r's smugness and me
causing a conflagrat
self-immo

An eight-year crime against humanity

Campaigners step up fight to close Guantanamo

Mo
b

he Hague, he took a
d Lansdowne Partner

absolutely everyor

ssianic tendencies

NOBEL ACCEPTANCE SPEECH

Warmonger picks up 'peace' prize

Obama quotes King in speech but sends 33,500 more troops to war

g at his blatant h
d by the breathtak

tember 11 to the 1

ight years ago.

this egregious c

But we won't

This week marked the first anniversary of the inauguration of US President Barack Obama. Twelve months on, his election cry of "Yes we can" is looking more like "Well, we could. But we probably won't."

Even the most faithful Obama flag-flyers are now shuffling their feet somewhat awkwardly and trying to look busy doing something else.

I'm sure many Star readers had the same reservations as I did amid all the frothing adulation with which Obama was elected.

But, to paraphrase the late great Linda Smith talking about Tony Blair, when it comes to Obama I had absolutely no expectations—and he still let me down.

Many, including me, would argue a large number who should have known better put great store in the hope provided by the Obama election.

For the record I do think he was onto a loser from the start. Trying to push through any kind of reform in a deeply conservative country where a significant minority still haven't got over the fact that black people are even allowed to vote, never mind become president, was always going to be difficult.

This is a country where the majority rely on Fox News for their information and apparently seem to think that foreign policy relates to Hawaii. It's a country where people bring assault rifles to health-care debates.

You have an anti-abortion lobby which is pro-death penalty and, as recently evidenced, doesn't always think it has to wait for a judge to OK it. These are probably the same nutjobs who have concluded, no doubt after exhaustive research—again, see Fox News—that the NHS is a death machine hell-bent on slaughtering pensioners.

"Free-ish health care for all? How dare he! It's some kind of pinko liberal socialist conspiracy," they bellowed.

But despite such wilful belligerence it shouldn't really have been that difficult to be better than George Bush, should it?

A semi-lobotomised chimp could have done as good a job of running the country as him. Some might argue that one did.

Yet in his first year what has Obama actually achieved? He got the Nobel peace prize for actually extending the war in Afghanistan—a smoke-and-mirrors act previously only carried off by Henry Kissinger, that doyen of foreign diplomacy.

Perhaps the most egregious example of the new president's pusillanimous backtracking on all the major issues was amply and graphically illustrated yesterday.

January 22 was the day that Guantanamo Bay was supposed to close its doors for good. Yet almost 200 men remain in legal limbo in the US concentration camp in the Caribbean.

Londoner Shaker Aamer is still languishing there despite having been cleared for release in 2007. Recent reports suggest that he may have been denied release because he has evidence of murder and torture at the base which could blow the lid on the whole horror show.

But then the US doesn't seem to care about world opinion on such trifling matters as the kidnap, torture and imprisonment without trial of wholly innocent individuals in their name.

Republicans went into raptures when former Cosmopolitan poster boy Scott Brown, who recently seized the Kennedy stronghold of Massachusetts, stated that, and I quote: "Water-boarding does not constitute torture when questioning terror suspects."

I'd like to see Senator Brown put his money where his mouth is and see if he still thinks waterboarding is OK after the boys from the CIA have had a little chat with him.

And while they're at it they could do a two-for-one and get Dick Cheney in as well. Now that would make a good Cosmo centrefold.

Monumental

as right to kill up
"really honestly" believe

William Hague
unveiled a
Westminster statue
to Ronald Reagan
with a fawning
homage to the
'greatness' and
'human touch'
of a man who
butchered his
way across
Latin America
having shopped
left-wing
members of his
own union to
the McCarthy
witch trials
during his
acting days

decided to rule ou
r's smugness and me
ausing a conflagrat
ng act of self-immo

nting the possibili
all re

US WAR CRIMINAL HONOURED IN LONDON

RONALD
WILSON
REAGAN

ssianic tendencies

g at his blatant h
d by the breathtak

tember 11 to the

ight years ago.

this egregious c

scumbags

Just when you think GB plc could not possibly kowtow any further to their US masters they show themselves to be more double-jointed than Olga Korbut.

I refer of course to the spectacularly crass decision to hoist an effigy of the late unlamented Ronald Reagan, not from the lamp post from which it should fittingly swing as so many opponents of Latin American dictators did, but in a place of honour in the metropolis.

It is informative to note that Westminster council broke its own rules to erect this monstrosity in double-quick time after Obi-Ron Kenobi shuffled off this mortal coil yet fought tooth and nail to remove a true hero of democracy in the shape of Brian Haw and his peace camp claiming it was an eyesore.

The sheer insanity of erecting a statue to a knee-jerk reactionary B-movie cowboy is bad enough, but then William Hague got up to speak...

Hague paid glowing homage from one war criminal to another, extolling Reagan's alleged virtues.

"Statues bring us face to face with our heroes," he chuntered—conveniently ignoring the fact that as it's 10 feet high it's more likely to bring him face to groin with the ex-prez.

"Ronald Reagan is without question a great American hero—one of America's finest sons, and a giant of 20th-century history."

He lauded the fact his "outstanding leadership qualities meant that even those who disagreed with his politics recognised his greatness."

Oh, really? Back in the real world—some way out of the orbit of planet hagiography—those who "disagreed" with Reagan's politics didn't seem to fare too well. Now maybe I'm being cynical and those slaughtered by Guatemalan death squads and butchered by the fascist Contras really did say: "Say what you want about Reagan—he's firm but fair."

Reagan of course was elected governor of California mainly due to scabbing and shopping left-wing members of the Screen Actors Guild to McCarthy and the House Un-American Activities Committee.

As president of the guild, Reagan used his position to smear and denigrate communists and socialists—and even those with no political affiliation—within the organisation for the betterment of his own career.

Reagan named names at the witch trials and ensured that large numbers of hard-working people were blacklisted and hounded—some of them to an early grave.

And this is the man Hague praised for "his extraordinary human touch." That's like praising Thatcher for her wonderful compassion towards the north of England.

There really is no limit to the extent the Tories are prepared to go in the name of the "special relationship." But, as has become very clear this week, even more than any other kind of relationship, when they go sour they go spectacularly sour.

Until this week it would not have been a surprise to see the Tories proposing a monument and fawning dedication to that other well-known union-busting scumbag—Rupert Murdoch.

It could have been a huge gold affair encrusted with jewels with Murdoch depicted bestriding Parliament Square and baring his buttocks in the direction of the House of Commons—with a smaller statue of David Cameron lodged firmly in its rectal cavity.

That now is unlikely to happen—although there's probably still some form of shrine in Tory headquarters where neophytes are forced to prostrate themselves and rub themselves with old editions of the Sun.

The professed outrage and shock from the Bullingdon boys over the phone hacking scandal is as laughable as Rebekah Brooks's denials of all knowledge of any wrongdoing.

In both cases they're either cretinuously incompetent or lying through their teeth.

s right to kill up
"really honestly" believe

Tea Party

A swarm of
religious bigots
came crawling out
of the woodwork
to gnaw away at
women's rights,
from the Republican
who wrecked his own
Senate campaign by
blabbering about
'legitimate rape'
to the Catholics
trying to sue Obama
to limit access to
birth control

decided to rule out
r's smugness and mel
ausing a conflagrat:
ng act of self-immo

nting the possibili
and confess all, re
devote the rest of

"adviser" to JP Mo:
s after he handed b;

he stand at an inqu
he Hague, he took a
d Lansdowne Partner

UNITED STATES
'Legitimate rape' congressman whips up storm

ssianic tendencies

g at his blatant h
d by the breathtak

tember 11 to the l

ght years ago.

this egregious c

Taliban

It's a good job we have all these experts when it comes to the issue of women's rights isn't it? And surprising that so many of them have found themselves in public office.

The issues of abortion and rape have been much in the news recently and there has been no shortage of middle-aged men happy to strut before the cameras and share their wisdom on the most serious of issues.

As usual in such matters the US right is very much at the head of the game.

In an interview with a St Louis TV station, Republican Missouri Senate nominee Todd Akin explained his rabidly anti-abortion stance by claiming that in instances of "legitimate rape" the female body shuts down, preventing unwanted pregnancy. Who knew he had majored in obstetrics?

And then there's that phrase "legitimate rape." Rape is a hate crime and by very definition cannot be "legitimate." To imply there is a gradation of offence is crass in the extreme.

Akin, who is, unsurprisingly, backed by the Tea Party psychos, backtracked shortly after by saying he "misspoke." There's been a lot of that recently. In fact every time one of these brain-dead zealots opens their gobs they "misspeak."

Someone who is clear he didn't misspeak, however, is Republican Party vice-presidential candidate Paul Ryan.

Ryan has, according to the San Francisco Chronicle, co-authored 38 anti-abortion measures including a number which would not make an exemption on the grounds of rape or incest.

He also voted for a ban on family planning funding in US aid abroad. Because let's face it all those HIV-infected African children just lack moral fibre. Akin—quelle surprise—supported every one of the 38 draconian measures.

Incidentally Ryan models himself as a great outdoorsman in the mythical US tradition, posing on horseback and rifle in hand with a variety of animals he has just slaughtered.

He also lists as one of his hobbies—and I kid you not—"catfish noodling." Which sounds like some form of strange aquatic perversion, like porpoise poking or dolphin dogging.

According to the redneck dictionary, it basically means strangling fish with your bare hands. And this is a man whose opinions are taken seriously by a large proportion of US citizens?

However, when it comes to reactionary bigots meddling with women's reproductive rights you can't beat the Catholic church. The church in the US is suing the Obama administration over its health-care plans, which would apparently mean employers—excluding houses of worship—having to provide free birth control through their health insurance.

The most senior US Catholic official, Cardinal Dolan, is apparently to give a benediction at the Republican National Convention next week, but claims this is not an endorsement of Mitt Romney.

His office said it was merely a matter of "a priest going to pray." So much for the separation of church and state...

"Never before," Cardinal Dolan said, "has the federal government forced individuals and organisations to go out into the marketplace and buy a product that violates their conscience."

And while we're on the subject of Cardinal Dolan, one might have thought he would have been keeping his head well below the parapet on any kind of "moral" issue at the moment.

You see it was his eminence who, while archbishop of Milwaukee in 2003, apparently presided over a policy of paying paedophile priests up to $20,000 to leave the priesthood.

Questioned over allegations that one particularly notorious paedophile cleric had been given a "payoff" to leave the priesthood, Cardinal Dolan responded that such an inference was "false, preposterous and unjust."

But earlier this year the archdiocese was forced to admit that such a policy did in fact exist and had been drawn up under ... Dolan. Apparently that was not in violation of his conscience.

hearing I had reluctantly decided to rule
sheer enormity of Blair's smugness and me
form of chain reaction causing a conflagrati
nd therefore an unwitting act of self-immo

did was try to link September 11 to the Ir
cular claim didn't hold water eight years a
evidence to support this egregious claim be

things were carried out mainly by

Lightning Source UK Ltd.
Milton Keynes UK
UKOW04f0951010514

230892UK00008B/39/P